We Don't Do that Tune, Vicar

'Reg Frary has been entertaining us for some 40 years with his humorous tales of mischievous choristers, vicars and organists, and judging by the number of books we have sold through RSCM, he has many fans.'
Church Music Quarterly

'His stories . . . are told with affection and wit.'
Methodist Recorder

'Frary takes the reader on a journey of brooding musical passions and intrigue . . . that will ring bells with anyone who has experience of a local church or village choir, whether having sung in one or endured the efforts of those who have tried.'
Church of England Newspaper

'. . . whimsical tales to amuse and entertain from a veteran storyteller.'
Christian Marketplace

We Don't Do that Tune, Vicar

More disharmony in the choir

Reginald Frary

CANTERBURY
PRESS
Norwich

In fond memory of a companion,
my cat Alfie, who appears in various
guises throughout my books
R.F.

© Reginald Frary 2007

First published in 2007 by the Canterbury Press Norwich
(a publishing imprint of Hymns Ancient & Modern Limited,
a registered charity)
13–17 Long Lane, London EC1A 9PN

www.scm-canterburypress.co.uk

British Library Cataloguing in Publication data

A catalogue record for this book is available
from the British Library

ISBN 978-1-85311-837-1

Typeset by Regent Typesetting, London
Printed and bound by
Bookmarque, Croydon, Surrey

Contents

Foreword

Words or Tune?

What makes a hymn popular – its words or tune? There have been times when the words seemed not to matter at all. During the latter part of the eighteenth century, in churches where many parishioners could hardly read, hymns had to be learned by heart so lines were necessarily few and simple. Some were hilarious, as in the case of the curious 'repeater' hymns, which were favourites sung with great vigour in country churches:

> O stir the stu-, stir the stu-,
> The stupid hearts of men.

and:

> I've caught my flee-, I've caught my flee-,
> I've caught my fleeting breath.

perhaps followed by:

> O what a mess-, O what a mess-,
> O what a messenger of love.

With these offerings it was indeed only the tune that mattered but in the case of some seventeenth-century hymns the words were all-important as warnings against every kind of ungodliness. Young girls who tended to become a little vain about their good looks were cautioned with the following:

When by spectators I am told
What beauty doth adorn me
Or in a glass when I behold
How sweetly God did form me
How God such comeliness display'd
And on me made to dwell
What pity such a pretty maid
As I should go to hell.

Another hymn from the same period sought to fix the story of Jonah's plight inside the whale firmly in the singer's mind:

Ah me! This is an awesome place
Without e'er coal or candle
Nothing but fishes' tripes to eat
And fishes' tripes to handle.

One of our noblest hymns, 'O God our Help in Ages Past', was written by Isaac Watts. It is strange to reflect, however, that this great and scholarly man also wrote a hymn with a verse that ran:

O lovely appearance of death
What sight in the world is so fair?
Not all the gay pageants that breathe
Can with a dead body compare.

Even more strange is the hymn he wrote for children, the first verse of which warned:

> There is a dreadful hell,
> And everlasting pains,
> There sinners must with devils dwell
> In darkness, fire and chains.

Words or tune? Cardinal Newman, when he wrote his verses beginning 'Lead, kindly Light', could have had no expectation that they would ever be sung, certainly no thought that they would become a hymn of vast, far-reaching popularity. But the poem caught the interest of a clergyman, John Bacchus Dykes, precentor of Durham Cathedral. He was also destined to become known as one of the most prolific and successful writers of hymn tunes of the nineteenth century, among whose most widely used tunes are those for 'Eternal Father, Strong to Save', 'Holy, holy, holy' and 'The King of Love my Shepherd is'. Dykes set Newman's verses to a tune that he called 'Lux Benigna' and a great hymn was born. It is said that Newman, whenever congratulated on his hymn, always attributed its success to Dykes' tune. Ironically the tune has now been largely replaced by less worthy and less suitable melodies.

One wet Sunday afternoon Sir Arthur Sullivan, the composer of the celebrated Gilbert and Sullivan operas, while visiting friends, was amusing the young daughters of the house by making up tunes and wheezing them out on a tiny harmonium. One of the tunes he fitted to a martial hymn recently written by a priest, Sabine Baring-Gould. The hymn was 'Onward Christian

Soldiers', and Sullivan's tune 'St Gertrude' has taken it round the world to wherever Christians sing together.

Millions are familiar with the stirring tune to which is sung Julia Ward Howe's 'Battle Hymn of the Republic'. In this case the words and music which have been sung at so many memorable occasions, including the funeral of Sir Winston Churchill, complement each other superbly – 'Mine Eyes Have Seen the Glory of the Coming of the Lord'. A verse evokes an extraordinarily vivid impression of the atmosphere in a Union army field camp during the American Civil War as a soldier meditates on the presence of his God:

> I have seen him in the watch fires of a hundred
>   circling camps;
> They have builded him an altar in the evening dews
>   and damps;
> I can read his righteous sentence in the dim and
>   flaring lamps;
> His day is marching on.

Serious opinion would say that the words of a hymn are more important than the tune. So be it. Yet the importance of a popular tune cannot be overstressed because it is often through a likeable melody that we are introduced to fine words which, had they been set to a less effective tune, might well have been overlooked by all but the discerning few.

Reginald Frary
Richmond
February 2007

1

Sir John and Fred

Although my friend George has been in his village church choir for over 40 years he's never reached the stage of singing a solo or even taking part in a quartet. He's remained perfectly happy as a member of 'the back row of the chorus' (he and another man who always sings half a tone flat and never finds the right hymn in the book until they're singing the third verse). It is the *history* of church choirs and musicians that so intrigues George. He's ever eager to pass on his knowledge to anyone who is interested.

On my recent visit to George he met me at the station with his huge, mud-spattered four-wheel drive car, a monster which always fills me with foreboding, especially when George is driving it. We set off smartly, neatly missing the vicar's wife and a friend who were gossiping in the middle of the road, and were soon hurtling between the hedges and ruts and holes of the unmade track towards the village that, at this point, I always wonder if we'll reach alive. Accelerating violently, George brilliantly circumvented a petrified rabbit and suddenly announced, 'Of course, in the early nineteenth century cathedral choirs were not as we know them today.' (He is in the habit of suddenly announcing things like that.) 'No, they were real ramshackle affairs. The choirmen – vicars choral – were often late for services or not there at all and the organist who was supposed to be in charge of training and rehearsal didn't like to upset them by insisting on anything like that.'

George careered around a larger than normal rut in the track at increasing speed and mud showered his windscreen. He continued, 'I reckon cathedral choirs in those days were just like our choir here still is today. Take St Paul's Cathedral for instance. Thomas Attwood was organist there in the early nineteenth century. Goodness knows how he managed the mob that were in the choir then. I can't find out much about his way of thinking about the choir. Anyway he was followed by John Goss. I always think Goss must have been a really nice man. I enjoy his anthems and like his famous hymn tunes – as long as they are not mucked about being re-harmonized by modern musicians who think they know better than Goss – how arrogant can you get? Goss was knighted, of course. In Victorian times you always got knighted if you took on a job like St Paul's choir. He used to say he was the only knight living in Brixton. He had a great sense of humour, which you needed as organist of St Paul's then. He kept his sense of humour, even when half the choir didn't turn up for a service. He merely encouraged those who *were* there to do what they could and he'd put the missing parts in on the organ.

'John Stainer was a choirboy at St Paul's in Goss's time and he remembered often watching the scuffles that took place at the vestry doorway between some choirmen and the vergers when a service had already started and the vergers were trying to stop the late choirmen slipping into the choir stalls and thus getting their pay. Stainer was a very different kind of man to the easy-going Goss. He followed Goss as organist at St Paul's but he only took on the job on the understanding that he ran the choir solely in his own way with no interference from the clergy. I think he was a martinet. They hadn't had one of those before. Anyway, the St Paul's people wanted him to take the job so they paid him a good bit more money than poor old Goss ever got and left him to it. Stainer took charge and turned the cathedral choir into one of the finest in Europe and it probably still is. He got knighted too. I reckon he deserved it.'

George halted his praise for Stainer for a brief space while he took a huge bite out of a generously filled cheese and pickle roll that had been bouncing about enticingly above the dashboard. He went on quickly, 'but, as I say, our choir here hasn't noticeably moved on like St Paul's has. It's just like St Paul's was in Goss's day only we haven't ever had anyone knighted. There *was* one of the organists in the 1860s who was made chairman of the parish council, but he never got any further towards being knighted. I reckon our present man wouldn't know what they were talking about if they tried to knight him. He'd probably think it was some new ruse they had thought up for boosting pop singers.'

But, despite being continually overlooked by the

compilers of honours lists, Fred the organist at George's church remains a delightfully cheerful person. In a way he's much like Sir John Goss at St Paul's must have been. He too, is ever ready to help out his choir by filling in on the organ the voice parts that are missing. Sometimes when the choir are performing one of Fred's favourite Victorian festival anthems, composed for massed choirs at the Crystal Palace, it is hardly possible to realize that they are managing with two tenors who only have the confidence to sing above a whisper when an occasional visiting tenor is bawling next to them, two basses, including George, who don't read music or take the slightest notice of marks of musical expression, a handful of very assorted sopranos and, as George puts it, a terrifying coven of blue-haired contralto ladies who have been there forever and dominate the whole set-up including the organist, the vicar and even the vicar's wife, a deceptively sweet and gentle looking lady who dominates everyone who isn't a contralto, with a will of iron.

On the unfortunately rare occasions that I visit George and join the village choir for choral evensong, the majority of the members are always most welcoming and friendly towards me and happy to assure me that nothing has altered in the parish since my last visit. They know that makes me feel at home. The village is indeed a very rare place in these chaotic days, a serene and secret place still mainly untouched by time's rude hand. I have a feeling though, that the contraltos don't like me very much. They don't know where to stand me in the choir stalls. Being a male alto I should, of course, sing with them but no one and nothing is allowed in the choir stall that they have made their own exclusively and I generally end up at the end of the row next to George who sings so boisterously throughout that it doesn't really matter what I sing. On this occasion, however, owing to a leisurely paced repair project being undertaken on one of the choir stalls, the whole choir were corralled in the other one and I found myself trapped in the midst of the feared contralto coven. The lady on one side of me, although not above average height, was one of those ladies who appear to be looking down on you from a great height. I think this one was standing on her hassock. 'We sing the last verse of each hymn in *unison*,' she hissed with a superior smile, 'and you are treading on my gown.'

I managed to get through the rest of the service without any further clumsy behaviour on my part and to my surprise my superior contralto neighbour sought further words with me in the vestry immediately after the service. 'You seem to come here regularly but at long intervals,' she observed as she cornered me in the cassock cupboard. 'We – my contralto colleagues and I – are planning a presentation to our organist in recognition of his 30 years' service to the church. He always tries to do his best and in the circumstances we can't expect more than that, I suppose. He's had no musical training – he started off playing the mouth organ I believe. Some of the choirmen had a *vague* idea of doing something for his twenty-fifth anniversary but – well – our choirmen are vague like that. We are nearing his thirtieth anniversary now and nothing whatsoever has been done so *we* are taking over. I take it that we may not be seeing you again for some time so if you'd like to contribute now ...'

I like Fred the organist. I said I'd be very pleased to contribute, which I did there and then, whereupon the lady released me from the cassock cupboard with a formal smile from on high and I was free to join George who was awaiting me in the churchyard, full of curiosity. 'You were highly honoured,' he declared in awesome tones when I explained my dalliance in the cassock cupboard. 'No one in the coven has mentioned a word to us men about a presentation to Fred. We thought of the idea first anyway when we suggested a celebration for his 25 years. We did talk about it quite a bit – we still do. These women are always in such an almighty *hurry* about everything ...'

Learning what the contraltos were planning to do about the organist's 30 years' celebration did at last spur on the choirmen. A secret meeting of the whole choir was quickly arranged to discuss what form of tribute to Fred would be best. Like other meetings in the parish it had to be kept secret, at least from the vicar's warden, a very cross young man with a high-pitched voice, who had the habit of virtually taking over gatherings from wedding parties to meetings of the PCC (generally reviewing the state of the permanent leak in the vestry roof) with his well-known tirade attacking clergy who don't wear clerical collars, bellringers who ring for hours and hours and stop the service from commencing on time, and people who block up the church porch after the service, shaking hands and chatting up the vicar and preventing others from escaping from the church as quickly as possible.

The choir met one Saturday evening in the back parlour of their favourite tavern, The World Turned Upside Down, the main seating, an ex-church pew, being occupied exclusively by the row of superior contralto ladies while other members perched about on a miscellany of stools and cosy seats made from old beer-barrels. The senior chorister, one of the whispering tenors, opened the meeting.

'Well, what are we going to do about him?' he asked.

'About our organist, Fred,' corrected the contralto spokeswoman.

'Yes, about him,' agreed the tenor. 'What are we going to do about him?'

One of the basses who is a teacher of English, who always likes to start a meeting on a humorous note added, 'Him wot plays the organ – the organ grinder.' The whole contralto row froze.

'Right, now let's begin,' said the other bass. 'Let's have some suggestions.'

The spokeswoman for the contralto coven spoke first. By common consent she always speaks first at choir meetings because what she says generally stirs up enough argument among members to comfortably occupy the major part of the meeting, particularly for those members who have loyally turned up without the faintest idea of what they want to argue about. 'My colleagues and I,' she eyed the line of contraltos in the pew like a general reviewing her troops, 'have come to the conclusion that the parish should demonstrate its appreciation of our organist's many years of service here by financing him to go on a basic course for organ students at the Academy.'

There followed what is sometimes referred to as a stunned silence, then one of the whispering tenors cleared his throat and said, 'Wouldn't he think that we were trying to be funny? You know, after 30 years of playing our organ?'

'Oh dear,' sighed the contralto. 'I can assure you he'd appreciate and be most grateful for our thoughtfulness.'

'I was thinking of something like a chiming clock,' said one of the assorted sopranos, 'or a new digital telly. The one he's got now is really past it.'

George suggested, 'Or what about a new bike? His old one is like his telly – past it. We could get him one with all those fancy gears.'

'Or what about a new armchair?' put in an older assorted soprano. 'Being a single man he doesn't see to things like that and that old chair of his must be awfully uncomfortable . . .' The meeting went on well into the night and nobody seemed to be getting anywhere.

George keeps me well in touch with the goings on in his choir; every few weeks he updates me on the phone. He's a very good reporter. 'So what eventually happened about Fred's presentation?' I asked when he rang recently.

'Ah, the contralto coven didn't get everything their own way,' he reported. 'There was a compromise. We bought Fred a new recording of an organ recital by a celebrated organist at the cathedral. I forget his name.

Fred had us all round to supper the other night to hear it.'

'Was it good?' I asked.

He hesitated, 'Yes it was alright – we didn't know any of the pieces but – yes, it was alright. But y'know, when I hear old Fred bashing out "The Arrival of the Queen of Sheba" at wedding services, or "The War March of the Priests" after Matins, I think there's nobody *quite* like our organist.'

2

The Feud

The village church where my friend Ernie sings in the choir and is also in the bell-ringing team, is most fortunate in these difficult times. As well as having an actual congregation who turn up regularly Sunday by Sunday – in addition to the midnight service on Christmas Eve – it also has the aforementioned choir (the only church choir for miles) who are always around, and the bell-ringing team.

Ernie told me, 'Well, we are a very lucky parish. There's always something going on. Lots of interest for everyone. All kinds of indoor and outdoor activities and we've well-attended study and organizing groups and there's what the vicar always enthusiastically refers to as the healthy exciting rivalry between the groups – well, rivalry anyway – like the rivalry between the choir and the bell-ringers – well, all-out feuding actually. So there's a reliable ongoing source of interest even if you're not a member of a group.'

No one now is quite sure what actually happened to cause the original choir versus bell-ringers feud but it had something to do with a wedding service that took place sometime back in the 1890s when the bells started ringing too soon at the end of the service and drowned out the choir who were singing the bride's favourite anthem. There have been other incidents between the choir and the bell-ringers down the years, of course, but the descendents of those partaking in the original incident have loyally maintained the spirit of the feud to this day.

Each year on the Sunday after the Christmas celebration services the vicar, in what Ernie calls his usual 'over-the-top ramblings', always thanks the choir (over and over again) in front of the whole congregation, for their year-long, splendid devoted efforts and everyone claps and shouts 'hear! hear!' and 'bravo' or 'for heaven's sake, let's get on with the service.'

But the vicar never mentions the bell-ringers. This omission seemed to have evaded the notice of the bell-ringers for years – probably, Ernie says, because most of them don't normally attend the service, instead retiring to The Dog and Duck immediately after their welcoming peal. This year, however, Ernie had made a fuss over the vicar's complete neglect of the bell-ringers and his 'cloying, soft-soaping of the choir'. Ernie is the one ringer who is also a member of the choir and thus has a foot in both warring camps. As a choirman he is quietly pleased, yea flattered, by the vicar's annual congratulations for the choir but noisily indignant over the vicar's annual 'calculated, insulting behaviour' in so obviously ignoring the bell-ringers.

It happened that the Sunday after the vicar's latest 'calculated insulting behaviour', I was on one of my rare visits to Ernie and his wife and found myself in the midst of the newest disturbance to fascinate the parish life of Ernie's ideal village. Being myself a campanologist, Ernie invited me to join the ringers for the Sunday morning service. When he and I arrived in the tower ringing chamber (with his wife's parting words to me ringing in our ears – 'Don't let him start anything. I'm sure that lot down at the church don't really go there to ring or sing. They only go there to aggravate each other and upset the vicar. They love it!') we were greeted by the outraged voice of the bell captain, a very large, round man with a brick red face who could have been anywhere between 45 and 60. He wore crumpled off-white tennis trousers suspended from wide multi-coloured braces that partially obscured a missive writ large across his T-shirt recommending somebody's 'Fine olde English cider'. He tramped back and forth among the other ringers with battered outsized trainers. He had obviously been listening to and heeding Ernie's earlier fuming about the vicar's misdeeds. 'Calculated, insulting behaviour', he was growling, 'calculated . . . insulting . . .' He seemed to relish the very sound of the words, ' calculated, absolutely calculated'.

We all stood around riveted for some moments by the bellicose bell captain. Then a large lady ringer wearing a sort of flamboyant gardening suit, wild pepper-and-salt hair and a determined expression cut in with, 'Come on you lot, let's leave all this till later in The Dog and Duck. We've only got five minutes before him on the organ starts blasting away and then that woman in the back pew'll start up moaning to the vicar that the bells and the organ are making such a racket that she can't meditate before the service.'

'Meditate!' gasped Ernie. 'Meditate! She stands just inside the porch door and catches everyone as they come in and does her best to get them to join a demonstration outside the vicarage against the dust on the pews or the small-print hymn books or the utter lack of chocolate digestive biscuits with the coffee after the family service.'

'And anyway,' supported the ringer in the gardening suit, 'it's the vicar who makes most noise before the service bellowing "Good morning" and "Hi there!" to everyone and shouting across people's heads that it's jolly good to see them back from their holidays.'

'Well, the poor vicar *has* to bellow,' defended a most attractive young woman, obviously a very new ringer who had not yet caught on to the ringers' current, official anti-vicar stance. 'The bells and the organ are always making such an unholy din just before the service.'

'Such an unholy din!' exploded the bell captain. 'Our bell ringers making such an unholy din? How dare you!'

'And him at the organ,' put in the big lady ringer in a suddenly conciliatory tone. 'He's only doing what he's supposed to do – playing the organ. If the vicar would only shut up guffawing and get that choir mob in some kind of order to process into church on time and in a civilized manner we'd all be better off.'

'Has anyone suggested anything like that to the vicar?' asked another ringer looking up from his Sunday paper whose banner headline took up the whole of the front page with the huge black words, 'STOP THIS SHAME!'

'It's no good doing that,' said Ernie. 'I tried it some weeks ago and he went red in the face and said we were all a happily united family so it was natural that we all greeted each other and laughed and talked when we arrived at church.'

'Him at the organ and the choir don't think they're in the happy united family,' said the Sunday paper man returning to his giant headline. 'They think the congregation are a bloomin' nuisance because they always sing flat and spoil everything.'

'We've really got nothing to do with this family thing, have we?' prompted the gardening suit lady. 'Well, you know . . . when we ask the church council for anything for the ringers, like a heater in the ringing chamber or a bit of carpet, they take not a blind bit of notice. The vicar is a bit different though. He's always quite polite when he says the church can't afford it.'

'Always polite, quite fatherly actually,' conceded Ernie. 'He never says no in a nasty way.'

'He never says no in *any* way to the choir,' rumbled the bell captain. 'New cassocks, new cushions in the choir stalls – they get the lot.'

The large ringer in the gardening suit was looking down into the church. 'That's done it,' she cut in urgently. 'The choir's coming in and there's no organ. We can't ring now. I wonder what's happened.'

The vicar bounced to the centre of the chancel and smiled his big vigorous smile. 'I'm sorry we've no organist at the moment, friends,' he roared. 'Our organist has just phoned. His car won't start. He's on his way on a bike. It is occasions like this that bring home to us how much – how very much – we depend on our wonderful organist and choir. How fortunate we are in this place to be able to so appreciate such a talented company.' He smiled enthusiastically, bowing to the choir. 'Now let us commence our service with the first hymn.' He paused momentarily, 'I don't think there were any bells this morning . . . Oh, well, . . . so the first hymn –'

The bell captain motioned us urgently to the ropes, a grim grin (if there is such a thing) on his face. 'Off we go then! Treble's gone!' he called and thunderously the bells took over, all enveloping. The vicar, choir and congregation looked round puzzled then gradually settled back in their pews. A man in the choir started to read *The News of the World* which he always brought with him to read during the sermon and someone in the congregation had a prolonged sneezing fit. A small girl escaped from her family in a front pew and skipped down the aisle talking excitedly into the ear of her stuffed elephant.

It was a short ring. After ten minutes it ceased abruptly. The vicar rose to the occasion. 'It is occasions like this that bring home to us how much – how very much – we depend on our wonderful bell-ringers. How fortunate we are in this place to be able to appreciate such a talented company.' He smiled enthusiastically, bowing in the direction of the bell-ringing chamber. 'Now, let us commence our service with the first hymn, "New Every Morning Is the Love".'

3

Grandfather at the Charge

On seeing the preserved head and tail of Ronald, Lord Cardigan's charger, who led the Charge of the Light Brigade at Balaclava, 1854.

Unlike most of my country friends, Alfie (named after a notorious, anarchical family cat) is not the village organist or even a member of the village choir – he is the vicar's warden, a gentleman with a great sense of humour that qualifies him so admirably for his job. 'Well you have to laugh, don't you?' Alfie chortled to me over the phone. 'Let me bring you up to date with our latest choir episode.'

The organist and choirmaster (one person) at Alfie's church is an easy-going, most accommodating young man as far as church music is concerned. He'll play anything at any time for anyone in return for the unlimited use of the church organ. Villagers hear him sometimes around midnight raging away with Wagner grand marches and other items like the grand march from *Aida*. He's very fond of grand marches.

But it's the organist's grandfather, an iron-willed octogenarian, still a very active member of the choir, who actually runs the choir. He's been around for so long that everybody – even the new forward thinking young vicar – tries to agree with everything he (forcefully) suggests. It saves time and ultimate frustration. Now, grandfather possesses meticulously kept records about the choir dating back over 150 years. The earlier ones were handed down to him by his grandfather who got them from an even earlier grandfather who, in addition to being a prominent member of the choir, was reported to have charged in the Charge of the Light Brigade at Balaclava in 1854.

His record apparently shows that as far as his singing voice was concerned he had none at all above a deep discordant growl. Nevertheless, he was a most highly respected member of the choir because he could handle a horse so superbly and he and his horse had actually got back from the Charge completely unscathed and subsequently these two had become the subject of the heavily stained-glass vestry window which represented horse and rider in full medieval armour and made the vestry rather gloomy on dull days but wonderfully romantic when the sun penetrated its carnival colours.

But back to the present – the current choir grandfather, having been impressed, yea greatly inspired, by seeing for the first time the British film, *The Charge of the Light Brigade* on television, was casting around for an extra target for the choir to achieve beyond singing at Sunday services and around the pubs at Christmas in aid of the old people's annual rave up in the village hall. He envisaged a target worthy of a choir with the glorious historical background of the Charge. With overflowing new-born enthusiasm and irresistible firmness he informed his grandson the organist and choirmaster that a sensational celebratory parish sing-along of famous warlike hymns all climaxing with Handel's 'Hallelujah' chorus must be organized, led by the massed village church choir, (always referred to as 'massed' at Christmas and Easter when the man from the garage and the post-mistress helped out the regular four approximate soprano ladies, the contralto who could double as a tenor at a pinch and the two thunder-ous 'football riot' basses together with the huddle of miscellaneous people who, during services, liked the idea of sitting in the choir stalls which were so much more comfortable than the congregation's new yellow plastic chairs that had recently replaced the pews (with nowhere to put your hymn book), with the vicar, of course, participating where the notes were not too high for him and he could manage to keep up.

At the next meeting of the Parochial Church Coun-cil, purely as a matter of courtesy, Grandfather sought the approval of his latest plans. Anything to do with Grandfather and the choir always rattles the PCC. No one knows quite how to respond and his frequent flights of fancy mesmerize them, sometimes until the early hours. In a determined effort to get away from this par-ticular meeting by half-past midnight at the latest, all the members listened dutifully open eyed and clapped vigorously as Grandfather at last sat down. In moments they'd passed a vote of thanks and the vicar had eagerly given the immediate go-ahead using his oft-repeated words to awkward people in the parish who had ideas and thoughts, 'Well done! Jolly good! Splendid!' and everybody escaped swiftly from the meeting bemusedly wondering what 'all that' was about.

The very next day Grandfather busied himself with his plans. First, he realized from past experience, it was essential to convince the whole massed choir that they could indeed rise to the occasion and display outstanding, if hitherto completely undetected, musical talent in performing at concert pitch with the brewery brass band and the organ. His method for doing this was not, however, to approach the singers as a whole. Choir members found themselves waylaid individually by Grandfather in supermarket, post office and pub and told how very good his or her voice was these days, how noticed and appreciated by the whole congregation. ('Only this morning our church school headmaster had said . . .', 'and the milkman just went on and on about you . . .', 'Talk about keen!')

Finally Grandfather requested any local professional singers to come forward to augment the massed choir. Two professional people, friends of Grandfather, took up the challenge. Their professionalism wasn't in singing however – one was a master carpenter and the other an expert in laying paving stones in patios. Grandfather had offered them both lucrative orders for carrying out work in and around his cottage together with a firm non-negotiable invitation to join the choir for the sensational sing-along. Both men were non-singers except at football matches but Grandfather was pleased that both were large, impressive-looking gentlemen who would be a great help in making the choir *look* like a distinguished one even if it didn't sound like one.

During the last few days before the big event Grandfather was seen to be going around with sprightly step and grim smile. His grandson the organist said there was no need to worry about the smile being grim. Grandfather always had a grim smile when he was happy. It was something to do with the bone structure of his face or that he had been successful again in 'putting one over' on the vicar by getting the choir to slip into the new-age family service some awful Victorian hymns that made the vicar shudder.

Then, for a short while, Grandfather's happiness was threatened. The vicar hardly ever looked back to old ideas – after all he *was* forward thinking – but having just glanced at the clutch of warlike hymns chosen for the sensational sing-along he brought himself to have a word with Grandfather and some choir members. 'You see,' he said in his kindly tone, used exclusively for very young and very old parishioners, 'all your hymns are about soldiers – men – and seem to be implying that only men are fit to be active Christians. In this hymn, "Stand up, Stand up for Jesus", for instance, there is no mention of women. In the days when this type of hymn was written there were no women soldiers.'

'Women *were with* the army though,' explained one of the football riot basses, 'they were in the Crimea at the time of the Charge of the Light Brigade – mostly wives and relatives of the soldiers – they did the camp washing and things.'

'Well now, have we got any poetesses in the village?'

wondered one of the approximate sopranos. 'If so, perhaps she could write an extra verse about women and slip it into the hymn.'

'We can't do that!' exclaimed the bass indignantly. 'This hymn is all very grand and heroic with trumpet calls and mighty conflicts. We can't slip in verses about women doing washing!'

The forward-thinking vicar plucked up courage. 'Perhaps we could change just this one hymn for something more representative of today's church,' he beamed encouragingly.

'We can't change it now, at the last minute,' began Grandfather, 'the band has got the music.'

The vicar was becoming insistent. 'The band are professional musicians, a change won't worry them.'

'And then there's the horses,' said the bandmaster, who was the driver of the brewery's remaining horse dray, 'they charged at Balaclava – hundreds of them. They were maimed and killed like the men, like they have been in all wars. We should have a verse about them. Don't you agree, Vicar?'

A look of complete puzzlement replaced the determined expression on the vicar's face. Even he, the young, forward-thinking vicar wasn't within a mile of thinking forwardly enough to envisage the Church eventually including God's lower creation in its worship. Abruptly he glanced at his watch as he moved away. 'Goodness, I must run. I'm interviewing a wedding couple in five minutes.'

So the evening of the sensational celebratory singalong inspired by Grandfather's rediscovery of the

Charge of the Light Brigade duly arrived and the brewery brass band publicized the event by marching from the brewery to the church to the huge brazen sounds of 'Colonel Bogey'. In the choir vestry Grandfather, resplendent in one of the choir's new powder-blue cassocks, was already directing singers where to sit in the choir stalls. On Sundays choir members sat where they fancied in the choir stalls, depending on whether they wanted to keep an eye on the congregation (who was sitting with who and which rebellious offspring was being given the longest rein to upset the members of the congregation who were without rebellious offspring) or remain hidden at the end of the row where they could relax and read the local paper during the sermon.

But this was a special occasion. With military precision Grandfather demanded of each arrival, 'tenor, or bass, soprano or contralto?' The choir members smiled good humouredly at the inquisitor, told him what voice they were, received the directions and seated themselves comfortably in their usual seats. A group of the choir members who were in the choir because they preferred the choir stalls to perching on the new plastic chairs were confronted with the vital voice question, 'tenor, bass, soprano or contralto?' They looked at Grandfather, bewildered, and said that they didn't think they were any of those – they were the choir . . .

The sensational sing-along was a great success. The massed choir mostly sang very well and the brewery band filled in when they didn't. Everyone in the large congregation enjoyed singing the famous tunes. Perhaps only the vicar pondered long on the actual *words* of the hymns, that so disregarded womankind. But he remained puzzled, almost annoyed at the bandmaster's plea that they should sing about horses, and in the age-old tradition of the Church, he totally ignored all thoughts of the rest of God's lower creation.

4

In a Mysterious Way

I hadn't seen or even heard of Arthur for years, in fact I'd completely forgotten him in the way one does after attending an office colleague's retirement party and promising enthusiastically, hand on heart, to keep in touch whatever happens.

In the midst of a London evening rush-hour the train ahead of my train had broken down and blocked the line as usual and, as usual, the driver of my train had kindly suggested that if we all wanted to get home by midnight we'd better get off his train and seek other means of public transport. From this particular station where we were marooned there *were* no other means of transport going in my direction and I was just fuming my way up on an escalator that wasn't working, groaning to myself that travel in London must have been faster and more reliable in the days of the stage coach, when a large lumpy figure blundered into me completely upsetting my equilibrium. Picking me up with a single huge heave that could easily have dislocated my shoulder, he started to apologize loudly. 'Just didn't see you old boy. Sort of ... hang on! Don't I know you? It *is* you – bloke with cats and been in a church choir for donkeys' years. Still around! Heavens!' He roared on for some moments, slapping me on the back with cheerful violence, and then we found ourselves in one of those establishments where they serve breakfast all day. Yes, he was indeed Arthur and after learning that I was still working and enjoying the experience and still in the choir, he roared 'Heavens!' again and eyed me incredulously. 'You don't look any different from when I saw you last – what, a dozen years ago.'

'Never mind my state of preservation,' I said. 'What's been happening to you? Still not married I suppose?'

'No,' he beamed. 'When I took early retirement I thought I needed a bit of peace and quiet, so, no, still not married.'

'Peace and quiet? You?' I echoed. 'How can you say such things? You *thrive* on lack of peace and quiet.'

Our all-day breakfasts arrived and there was a silence while we dealt with them. But Arthur could never stay silent for long. 'I,' he proclaimed grandly, 'I am a new man. I've turned my back on the pubs and clubs of polluted City life, sold both my vintage sports cars and bought a pedal bike, a horse and a couple of golden retrievers and live in a tarted up, listed Victorian hovel in an undersized village, in the middle of nowhere – well, Suffolk actually.'

I suppose I would have replied that I was speechless but as I *was* speechless he carried on unimpeded. 'There's no pub in the village, they've closed the post office and they haven't got a cricket or football team so all the colourful local life is concentrated around the village church. So I go to church every

Sunday – and now I'm a leading member of the choir.'

'When you were at the office,' I stuttered confusedly, 'the only time you'd been inside a church was at your christening and I suppose you couldn't have very well got out of that – and further, I didn't know you could sing at all!'

'Neither did I,' he assured me. 'It was a vicar who pointed it out to me at my old aunt's funeral. I was her only living relative. She left me the listed Victorian hovel, y'see. That's how I got to live in the village. We sang "Abide with me" at the service and I remembered *that* one from school so I sort of joined in loudly.'

'I must be dreaming,' I interjected.

'No you aren't,' he said. 'Anyway, after the funeral the vicar invited me to the vicarage for a drink. He seemed quite excited and said it was a joy to hear me singing so beautifully and with a voice like mine I simply must join the choir. He reckoned the choir were very short of tenors, in fact they hadn't got any tenors at all and I'd make all the difference especially on the Sundays the other choirman, the bass, didn't turn up.'

My amazement was still growing. 'So you've actually moved into this remote outpost and joined the choir wherein you sing a beautiful tenor with a bit of bass on the side,' I summed up.

'That's right,' he confirmed '– best day's work I've ever done.'

'So what's this isolated band of singers really like?' I asked.

Arthur smiled. 'I don't know really,' he said. 'Not being musical, it's hard to say, but sometimes when we have a well-known hymn we absolutely *drown* the organ. It's all most enjoyable, very *robust*, so we must be pretty good, I mean – to drown the organ!'

'And what about the organist?' I enquired. 'Does he mind being drowned every time the choir knows the hymn.'

'A great character is Fred,' Arthur enthused. 'The story is that he's the only one who can manage the organ. No one else in the church understands it. It's a right mischievous animal, I can tell you – some say it's haunted – but on a good day Fred can make it sound really impressive. His favourite piece is Verdi's "Grand March" from *Aida*. He plays it every chance he gets – weddings, funerals, christenings, animal services, meditation gatherings – he says he's introducing grand opera to the masses.'

'And what do the masses in the congregation think of that?' I asked.

'They love it,' he affirmed, '– well no one has actually *complained* and everyone goes home from the service humming or whistling the tune, happy and carefree y'see – no matter what vital questions for urgent, serious consideration and meditation the vicar has raised in his sermon.'

'Ah, the vicar,' I said. 'What is he like?'

Arthur had a ready picture. 'Nice old boy, bachelor, tall, elegant, always wears his clerical collar and a monocle wherever he goes. Main thing about him is his wonderful speaking voice – absolutely Shakespearian.

We could listen to him for *hours* – generally *have* to anyway, every Sunday morning at the family service. He goes on for quite a bit in the sermon. He's a top theologian, I'm told, and most of us are never quite sure what he's talking about but it's an experience just listening to those mellifluous tones flowing over us . . .'

When Arthur and I parted after the all-day breakfast that evening it had been arranged that I should spend a weekend at Arthur's Suffolk retreat and, of course, join the choir for Sunday service. On Sunday morning a week or two later Arthur and I entered the choir vestry through a partially hidden doorway at the back of the village church whose thousand-year-old walls were so thick that it appeared we were walking into a cave cut out of massive rock. It seemed that the often absent bass was indeed present this morning. He was sitting in a corner perusing a copy of *The News of the World* and exclaiming, 'Disgusting! Unbelievable!' but as he saw us he strode forward smartly grabbing my hand in a paralyzing grip and informed me in a deep rumble, 'We do *Ancient and Modern* here and *The New Cathedral Psalter.*'

'Great stuff,' I said. I agreed with him absolutely and he pumped my hand again and moved back into his corner and *The News of the World*.

Gathered around a large gilded 'antique' mirror, still bearing its 'reduced to clear' sticker, half a dozen red-robed young women choristers were adding final touches to their appearances. Standing clear of them was one of more mature years and darkly forbidding mien who I guessed was the contralto. Arthur, seem-

28

ingly concerned about the forbidding mien, whispered urgently to me that Irma only *looked* like that – it was the way she did her hair and sometimes the tinting went a bit wrong – but in reality she was a very pleasant person and a wonderful cook who provided the most delicious provender for frequent choir suppers – and brewed parsnip wine which was out of this world. Arthur introduced me to her as an old acquaintance of his worldly days in the City. I don't know whether this information made me, in her eyes, an unwelcome tempter from Arthur's regrettable past but she gave me only a very distant nod and ghost of a smile while glancing with obvious distaste at my new yellow tie which had been given to me as a birthday gift by a trendy lady in my parish in an effort, no doubt, to modernize my image as a partaker in the vicar's get-away-from-formality, new family service.

Arthur moved me on, rather hurriedly, I thought, to the younger lady sopranos who were decidedly more charming – one said that it was nice to have two and a half men in the choir this Sunday instead of the one and a half men on who they usually had to rely. The bass, she explained, only counted as half a man as he only appeared in the choir stalls half the time.

Irma, the contralto, pushed her way through the group of sopranos to the piano on which Arthur and I leaned in conversation. 'You'll want a cassock and surplice,' she instructed me. 'Come over here.' She snatched a cassock from the robes cupboard which I caught neatly as she tossed it at me. 'No,' she shouted before I'd got it fully on, 'too baggy. We can't have that.'

'It's quite all right really,' I sought to reassure her. 'It's fine.'

'It's baggy,' she repeated. 'Here, grab this one. It will fit perfectly,' and she turned to supervise Arthur in the art of donning his cassock and surplice. 'Why do you always look as though a hurricane has hit you?' she asked him. 'There, that's better, but stand *up*. You can't sing crumpled up like that,' and Arthur quickly came to attention.

The actual service went quite well, I thought. It was one of those affairs where you never know what is going to happen next, so you are constantly on the alert and the vicar doesn't preach from the pulpit but, in Arthur's words, spreads himself around the whole congregation ready to hustle any member who, despite the charm of the preacher's voice and the importance of the message, may be drifting away after the first fifteen minutes. The proceedings – which resolved themselves into a sort of ebullient hymn sandwich – concluded with a spirited rendering of 'Stand up! Stand up for Jesus' (organ drowned) and after the blessing, having rather lost themselves in Stainer's 'Sevenfold Amen', the choir left the choir stalls at a quick shuffle into the vestry where the vicar adapted his famous mellifluous voice to rattle through the choir dismissal prayer before anyone could divest themselves of their robes and make for the Sunday lunch hospitality at The Goat and Compasses.

Arthur had reserved a table for the two of us in an un-believably rustic corner of the dining room that housed a fine pair of stocks – which enhanced the welcoming atmosphere most vividly of course. He beamed. 'This is the life, what! This church choir world is nothing short of wonderful.'

'How long have you been part of it?' I asked.

'All of three months,' he assured me, 'and that takes in Christmas. It becomes more fascinating every day. There is that funny sort of camaraderie with all these odd people connected with the choir. There's the vicar, a very nice man. You might not grasp what he's saying in his sermons but he's spot on when he's having a go at the organist. Those two never seem to agree about hymns but they're the greatest buddies in the pub darts team.'

'How do you rate your colleagues who are actually in the choir?' I encouraged him.

'Well, there's the sopranos of course,' he smiled. 'They are all youngish and attractive – just what is needed in the front choir stalls to keep the choir *noticed* – one or two of them can read music too.' He chuckled softly. 'Then there's the bass gent who pops up now and again.'

'The half bass,' I amended.

'Yes, him,' he agreed. 'I wonder where they got him and if he ever sings the right words to the tune. He really enjoys himself though. He adds to the enjoyment of all, as the vicar says. And he's a very nice person. He dug out an almost new cassock for me last week. The one they first gave me only has one button.'

'Ah, that's an old choir joke,' I explained. 'Most choirs – well your sort of choirs – work something like that on visitors. It's all part of the choir tradition.'

'And is it part of tradition for the congregation to actually *like* the choir?' he asked.

'Oh yes,' I explained. 'If they had no choir there'd be so much less for them to complain about to the vicar's church council.'

Arthur's manner became almost secretive. 'And our contralto lady who's always shouting at people and pushing them around. Do most choirs always have one of those too?'

'Oh yes,' I assured him. 'There's always one of them – sometimes two. They add character to the choir and keep everyone on their toes!'

'She's a person after my own heart,' Arthur declared. 'Knows her own mind and speaks it – well, shouts it sometimes. Yes, I appreciate her. I've never met anyone quite like her.'

'No, well, you haven't been in many church choirs yet have you?' I reminded him.

He shook his head. 'No, but I'm sure there's no one like her.'

Three months later I received an invitation to sing in the choir at Arthur and Irma's wedding. Arthur's old aunt who left him the listed Victorian hovel would have been overjoyed, I'm sure, to know how things had turned out. Suddenly I began to wonder. Was *she*, with the vicar, behind the whole story? I'd seen her newish, very descriptive memorial tablet in the chancel. She too had been a contralto in the choir, where there had been an unbroken family connection for two hundred years. The show must go on.

5

In the Churchyard

My bachelor cousin Sydney lives in Suffolk, in one of those friendly, nineteenth-century terrace houses which press so tightly together that if you want to walk more than a few steps inside, you have to build extensions on to the back.

In the case of Sydney's house, the extensions have been carried out on a grand scale. They are built of every material and in every style you can think of, and they extend over halfway down the back garden, ending up with a sort of outsize wooden dog kennel which is really a wash-house, which can't be used because it's crammed with lumber that has gradually filtered through all the other extensions and can't get any further. Sydney reckons that there is a washing machine still in there somewhere, and a tap and sink, but he hasn't seen them for years.

He has got some really splendid ideas about the cultivation of the remaining fragment of the back garden. He's had them for years. He reads all the gardening magazines from cover to cover, and buys everything that they recommend for the smaller garden. In fact, he's got so many sacks of fertilizer and cement, piles of crazy paving and disintegrating boxes of plants and wrought-iron gates and fences all over the place that he can't see the ground at all. And matters haven't been improved recently by the pompous presence of four magnificent white and gold ballroom doors, salvaged from a demolished Victorian mansion for the purpose of making a shed to protect the super electric lawn-mower and vast collection of gardening tools which Sydney has amassed on the expert advice of gardening magazines.

Apart from thinking about gardening, Sydney has only one other real interest. When he is not lovingly contemplating the chaos in his backyard and fixing in his mind the position of the ornamental goldfish pond, or visualizing the fragrant banks of roses that will bloom throughout the summer round the dustbins and the disused coal bunker, he is playing the organ at the village church.

His enthusiasm is tremendous. Not only does he play for the services, he is also very fond of playing at around 2 o'clock in the morning, and at one time the vicar, who lives next door to the church, used to get quite nasty about his being regularly wakened at that hour with the 'War March of the Priests' or the 'Trumpet Voluntary'. In fact there is no doubt that he would have taken what he referred to at a church council meeting as 'very definite steps', had not the church council reminded him that if they upset Sydney and he went off in a huff, they'd never get another organist – at least, not one who could make the organ work. As one church councillor who had been a member of the choir for 60 years emphasized, the last time anyone checked over the organ was the year he joined the choir. The organ builder had warned them then that it was on its last legs, so goodness knew what they'd find and what it would cost if they opened it up now. After all, Sydney knew exactly where to kick or thump it, but a new man wouldn't have the faintest idea, and would probably start demanding a complete overhaul or something ridiculous like that.

So the vicar, considerably chastened and not a little appalled at the awful prospect of being landed with a new organist completely devoid of the knowledge of where to kick and thump the organ, graciously withdrew his complaint and obtained some earplugs, which he kept handy on his bedside table.

During my first visit to the village, Sydney took me along to the church, a delightful little thatched-roof affair of incredible age and, for the most part, surrounded by dozens of giant memorial stones which leaned drunkenly in all directions, or just lay on the ground. A considerable portion of the churchyard had, however, surprisingly remained grave-free. It fronted the choir vestry and in the middle of it, in line with the vestry door, was a tall, rusty iron gate. At one time, I imagine, it was set in a dividing fence or hedge but this had long since disappeared, leaving it now quite on its own. In my ignorance I walked round the gate to the vestry door – and immediately recognized my error. Sydney was very deliberately passing through the gateway.

'It's the right way,' he explained. 'It saves the garden from being trampled over.' He latched the gate

ceremoniously behind him, and we both stood contemplating the 'garden'. 'I've told the vicar I'll take it
over and make some improvement,' he explained. He
indicated a fine, flourishing growth of dock leaves and
dandelions. 'I'm going to have bush roses there, and just
here' – he gave me a helping hand over a pile of broken
paving stones, the remains of a concrete coal bunker
and a chimney pot – 'I'm going to build a rockery.
Always attractive, a rockery. I'm going to get all the
choirboys on the job. I've got big ideas for this.' He led
the way into the vestry.

'Look at this,' he enthused, piloting me towards a
darkly forbidding corner between a cracked, black
iron stove held together with wire, and a stone bust of
a gentleman who at some time seemed to have lost his
nose, and had gained a rather evil looking cloth cap
which he wore at a particularly rakish angle. Sydney
pointed to a long brown photograph suspended from
a nail in the wall. 'Taken in 1880,' he announced
reverently. 'The ground outside this vestry has *always*
been a garden. This is an actual photo of choirboys
working on it all those years ago.'

I studied the photograph closely. It showed a collection
of extraordinarily villainous-looking urchins standing
about amidst piles of mud and uprooted shrubs. Also in
the ensemble was a large Victorian vicar, accompanied
by what was obviously an even larger Victorian vicar's
wife. The vicar appeared like most Victorian vicars in
photographs, gazing glassily ahead like something out
of a waxworks exhibition, but his wife, splendidly supporting a sort of dinner-plate hat entirely covered with

stuffed birds and wax cherries, looked very lifelike, and was glaring in a most regal manner at the urchins and the piles of mud. And in the forefront, a little out of focus and blotting out a good third of the picture, stood the iron gate.

Later, as we carefully picked our way through the dandelions and broken builders' material and continued correctly through the iron gate, Sydney told me what was one more story of the sheer inhumanity and gross ignorance of church councils.

He gazed proudly at the wilderness around us. 'You *love* tradition,' he told me. 'You'll appreciate what I'm up against. This has *always* been a garden for the free enjoyment of all, and I've got plans to make it even better. Yet, do you know what the church council wants to do now? They want to build a parish hall on it. A *parish hall!*' He seemed incredulous at his own words. 'Can you imagine it?'

I tried to cheer him. 'Well, perhaps at least they could use the iron gate outside the main entrance of the hall,' I suggested brightly. 'It might look all right patched up here and there and painted over.'

Sydney did not deign to reply to this inanity. 'All over the country, church tradition is dying,' he declared, putting one foot on the relegated chimney pot and addressing himself to a forlorn hollyhock in a sea of stinging nettles. 'All the people at the top want to do is change everything – a new Bible, new sorts of services, new tunes to the hymns – even new *hymns* – and they call them songs! And now they want to build on our vestry garden. No wonder the churches are half empty.'

They haven't built the parish hall yet. There seems to be a question of money, and the church council has been hard at it discussing ways and means of raising some these last five years.

Sydney of course, continues to lay his plans to improve the vestry garden. It's not going to have bush roses where the docks and dandelions are, after all. Instead, there's going to be an oak seat so that the old folk can sit and enjoy the flower beds. This will involve moving the broken paving stones, but they will be used to make a rambling path to the iron gate, bordered on both sides by a profusion of delightful blooms.

Meanwhile, Sydney's own garden had become a little too well stocked with the recommendations of the gardening magazines, and recently the position was reached where he couldn't get out of his back door owing to the arrival of a lorry-load of the very latest fertilizer and the parts for a do-it-yourself greenhouse. So Sydney has moved a quantity of the stuff up to the vestry garden (only until he gets going on his plans, of course), and now the only possible way to reach the vestry door *is* through the iron gate.

6

A Real Family Service

They were breaking in a new vicar at the Berkshire village church where my Auntie Rosie sings in the choir. Rosie has been in the choir almost as long as the old vicar, a happy bachelor, had been at the church. And very few people could remember when he hadn't been there. He and his vintage motor cycle and sidecar were part of the very fabric of the village. But now, at an undisclosed advanced age, he'd retired and moved to Derbyshire to join a brother of even more advanced age in his hill climbing activities.

The new vicar, a recently married young woman full of enthusiasm and dozens of ideas for radical change in the parish that nobody wanted to know about, was carrying on undaunted, serenely sure that her ideas were right and would therefore eventually succeed. To her sorrow, however, she had to admit that a sizeable portion of the congregation, led by the choir, had made it quite clear to her that they didn't want to be messed about with any of her 'thrilling new thinking' about Sunday services. They knew exactly what they liked, had always liked and intended to go on liking. It was, for instance, simply no good the vicar going on about introducing her relevant-to-today, meaningful 'praise songs' concerning chummy, caring communities and happy industrial relations to replace favourite Victorian hymns about angel choirs and heavenly Jerusalems.

The vicar was secretly worried about the impression her church was creating in a rapidly changing Anglican world and especially in the neighbouring village church where all was light and joy and hand-shaking and hugging and no one had ever heard of the Book of Common Prayer. It was all such a great pity, this ignoring of the vicar's wishes. She freely admitted that her congregation were a splendid crowd at bottom, fiercely loyal to the Church, widely active in all good works, generous, cheerful. But when it came to Sunday services, although there were reasonable attendances at the modern Family Service, there was this underlying lot who would insist on carrying on with these awful formal services with yards of four-square psalms and canticles that no one but the choir could sing and, of course, the aforesaid hymns about angels and heavenly Jerusalems.

And it was indeed with hymns that the new vicar was most concerned. She had, waiting in the wings, a large paperback volume of new 'praise songs' that she was bursting to introduce into the church services as soon as she could inveigle the choir into looking at it. And the best way to tackle the choir, she thought, was to get really chummy with their most influential member, who was undoubtedly Rosie. Wasting no time in accomplishing this pleasant state she embarked on tactics well known to her kind. From various willing sources in the local post office and pub, she sought to discover Rosie's main interests and pastimes apart from her choir activities. The trouble was that Rosie's only other absorbing interest was cats – she has three huge, round, identical tabbies who only she can tell apart – while the extent of the new vicar's knowledge about cats was that they were things that dug up her carrots and made a row at night. But, as had been said, she was an undaunted, serenely sure character and she pushed on eagerly with her plan. Every time she waylaid Aunt Rosie in the village street or trapped her in the coffee room after the Sunday morning Family Service she beamed at her and asked how the cats were.

She blundered. Far from producing the required chummy atmosphere between them, this only annoyed Rosie more and more because she was fed up saying, 'Oh! Fine Vicar, just fine' – and this was all she *could* say about them because they were always in the peak of condition and never did anything but loll about all over the place looking magnificent.

Aunt Rosie is, however, a very polite person and her façade of pleasure at the vicar's continuous concern for her cats was flawless. Thus, after a few weeks the vicar considered that the time was ripe to introduce to her the subject of 'praise songs'.

She trod carefully. One Sunday morning at coffee she bounced up to Rosie and asked the usual caring question about her cats but before she could give the usual appreciative answer the vicar said that just for a bit of variety didn't she think it would be quite fun for the choir to try out one or two really relevant new hymns (she prided herself on her caution in using the word 'hymns' instead of 'praise songs' – that could come later) from a really lovely book that she had recently come across? Rosie replied that as long as she kept the things *strictly* to the Family Service where everybody seemed to do just what they liked anyway and the chaos altered from week to week, and she didn't start messing up *proper* services like choral Matins and Evensong with them, she was sure the choir couldn't care less. And the cats were fine, just fine, thank you. And the vicar said 'Good! Splendid! Grand!' but wasn't quite sure whether she'd scored a point or not.

It was about this time that I paid one of my regrettably infrequent visits to Aunt Rosie. On these occasions the proceedings at her eighteenth-century cottage, 'The Cubby Hole', are always cosily familiar. Aunt Rosie produces an abundance of home-made hot buttered scones and a generous pot of beverage that she calls real tea, the like of which I have never been able to produce with London water even with the most exclusive tea bags. She then looks me up and down, asks if I'm *sure* I'm eating enough and sleeping well and goes on to tell me all that has happened in the village since my last visit. In reality very little does happen – the village doesn't move with the times. Indeed it remains as it was 50 years ago, so Rosie's bulletins are mostly repetitive. But they are never dull. The old vicar used to say that she could make a visit to the village shop for six eggs a sensational story. However, this time there *was* a new topic – an in-depth assessment of the new vicar. Aunt Rosie spoke for minutes in the manner of a form mistress reporting to parents as kindly as she possibly could, on the prospects of a well-below-average pupil. She concluded optimistically, 'She's as stubborn as any man but I'm sure she *can* be led. In the right hands I don't think she'll be much trouble at all. True, she's got the odd fixation about her book of doggerel – her "praise songs" – but then *all* vicars have some kind of eccentricity, I find, and we can get round this one easily by agreeing to sing her stuff at the Family Service. It'll probably go well with dancing in the aisles which I'm sure is coming next.'

Well, unconventional happenings were already occurring at the new vicar's Family Service and the Sunday of my visit to Aunt Rosie was no exception. As I neared the choir vestry door – I have a standing invitation to join the choir during my visits – two excited little girls with saucer-round eyes scampered into my path and squeaked, 'There's all lions and tigers in the vestry.' And one of them added shrilly, 'and Helephants!'

'And Helephants!' I gasped. 'We must see about this.'

And indeed the place was a chaos of roaring, trumpeting choirboys all wearing pantomime animal skins and papier-mâché heads. 'Our wildlife support effort – the whole collection will go to conservation projects,' beamed the vicar from the midst of the scrum, and the uproar increased rapidly until the organist, an austere figure, apparelled as always in an immaculate grey pinstripe suit, appeared from nowhere, lifted the heads off two of the most ferocious tigers and explained to them in cultured tones that unless they desisted immediately

43

he would personally eject them to the churchyard from whence they would be utterly precluded from entering into the imminent junketings in the church. He then reminded the rest of the menagerie that they were still required, nay, ordered, to sing throughout the service as human beings. The gentlemen of the choir would, of course, don their usual cassocks and surplices and remain human and do their best to keep things civilized. The vicar said, 'Great, Splendid!' and kept on beaming, the organist disappeared into the organ and we all herded into the church in front of a packed congregation. I didn't see any lions or tigers or elephants among them but I did spot a curiously hollow-backed zebra and there was a gorilla handing out the service leaflets whose coat looked like a discarded hearth rug and who wore the highly polished shoes of the retired major who usually took up the collection.

Like the hollow-backed zebra the service had no particular shape as far as I could discern, but we kept on singing things from the vicar's praise song book accompanied by, I think, a buffalo and a sort of crocodile who were beating drums out of time with the choir who were out of time with the organ. Then the vicar ambled up and down the main aisle saying what seemed some very inspiring things although I couldn't hear her actual words because the relay system in the choir stalls had gone wrong and everything sounded like a railway-station announcement.

Finally we did sing something I recognized – 'All Things Bright and Beautiful' – while the collection was taken. There was so much to collect that the gorilla with the shiny shoes had to call on the sort of crocodile to assist him and we sang the last two verses of the hymn again while we waited for them.

Later, safe in the serene orderliness of choral Matins, I reflected on the Family Service Wildlife romp. The vicar was in ecstasies because the choir had actually used her new praise song book, the wildlife societies would certainly be delighted with what was in the gorilla's plate and I was happy indeed that the affair was an occasion, although, sadly a very rare one, when the Church actually acknowledged that Christians should care, not selfishly only for humankind, but also for the rest of God's creation that shares this world with us and is in our care. That had been a *real* Family Service.

7

The People Opposite

The station was a large and very busy one on the main line to London. I stood on Platform 2, on my way home from a famous agricultural show which I had visited solely to see the Shire horses. I had seen those magnificent creatures – dozens of them. I had noticed little else. I felt very happy, very proud that England produced the greatest horses in the world. I still noticed little else.

But I *was* confident that I was on the right platform.

I gradually became aware of a loud-speaker. It was bawling something about a train that wasn't there and wasn't likely to be there. There were some long complicated, and mainly unintelligible instructions which sent people scurrying to all the other platforms where there were also no trains, or where the trains they wanted had just gone, or just hadn't stopped. I gathered that I was required to go to Platform 4 and, over there, I asked a smart young porter when my train was coming. 'Soon now, sir,' he assured me brightly. He surveyed the hordes of would-be passengers who were wandering all over the platforms like lost sheep. 'There's been a little bit of trouble up the line with a derailed goods truck,' he explained, 'but things will clear in no time now,

I'm sure sir.' He smiled encouragingly and walked on briskly to lull the suspicions of other lost sheep.

Almost immediately, an incredibly ancient and filthy diesel locomotive hurried through the station in a cloud of black fumes pulling a string of trucks marked 'Bananas' and 'Empty to Birmingham'. The smart young porter called back. 'There you are, sir. Things are moving again now.' I appreciated his cheerful optimism and thanked him, and said I was very pleased.

Long afterwards, when I had visited the station snack bar six times and coaxed the last packet of nuts and raisins from an automatic machine, the London train arrived. The big snub-nosed diesel lumbered over the points and drew its carriages slowly along Platform 4 where it ground to a standstill at one end, and stood emitting dangerous little snuffling noises like a bad-tempered bulldog. I had a strong premonition that somehow this was not going to be a very peaceful journey.

It was one of those one-compartment type trains with seats facing each other across little tables. I chose an empty seat and settled myself by the window. A surging tide of people began to flow by. In the manner of such tides they were all gazing desperately for some non-existent seats far ahead, and having found they were not there, they all flowed back again and trickled into the seats which they could have had in the first place, without the effort of tramping through the entire train. The party that trickled round the table where I sat consisted of a very large lady with two boys of about nine and three years. The large lady dumped a miscellaneous col'ection of hold-alls, brown-paper parcels, toy fishing rods and the boy of three, all over the table in front of me, and told me I didn't mind, did I? The elder boy was already standing on the seat opposite me, and appeared to be sticking green wine gums on the window. He said he didn't like the taste of the green ones.

Mum leaned across and knocked the wine gums off the window from where they fell stickily on to the seat. She then cuffed the boy and ordered him to sit down which he did, right on the wine gums. She appealed to me with a beautiful, spontaneous smile. 'You'd never think he was a choirboy, would you?' she said. I assured her that under his very natural exuberance, I was sure he was just the type, and she warmed to me instantly. She carefully squeezed into the seat beside me.

At this point the head of the family arrived in the form of another very large person, heaving a tray full of potato crisps, two cups of fine old railway coffee, and two bottles of highly dangerous-looking coloured stuff. These last he handed to his offspring and told them to drink it slowly and not bloomin' well choke themselves.

'Yes,' continued Mum, when Dad had heaved himself into the opposite seat and knocked half his coffee into a hold-all, 'our vicar is a funny type. Always *on* to our Alfie. Always *down* on him just because he's a little high spirited. Well, I meantersay, boys will be boys, won't they? And anyway, he's got the best voice in the choir.' She appealed eagerly to her husband. 'Hasn't he, Fred?'

''Opeless 'e is,' pronounced Dad, staring blankly at the front page of a famous newspaper which was all

48

headlines and pictures and no reading matter, 'dead 'opeless. Can't sing a note. Just like me.' He put down the paper and spoke earnestly, as if endeavouring to overcome my incredulity. 'It's a fact,' he said. 'I can't sing a note.'

Mum carried on with unabated pride, 'and he helps the church in other ways too. Why, although I say it myself, he put up six stalls for the garden fête last month before the other choirboys had put up one.'

'That's right,' agreed Dad from behind the next page of the famous newspaper, which still contained no reading matter, 'and five of 'em fell down before he got the sixth one up. Useless! Not like me there. Less haste, more speed is what I always say.'

I was so engrossed now that I failed to notice the ticket collector until he demanded threateningly, 'Tickets!' I was so flustered that I made matters worse by offering him a return half of an underground ticket to Cockfosters which had been in my wallet for 18 months. At this, his threatening attitude turned to one of pity. 'No sir,' he explained gently, 'this is the one.' And he picked up my ticket which was right in front of me on the only clear square inch among the debris on the table.

We now drew into a station – I forget its name, but I remember it sounded something like Retarded – where a porter, wearing a pullover full of holes, and a cap with a sunflower stuck in it, welcomed the alighting passengers in the dignified manner of an usher at a court ball. As the train moved off again, Alfie made a rude face at a saintly-looking old clergyman on the platform and to my surprise the saintly-looking old clergyman made a rude face back.

'Alfie's singing "O for the Wings of a Dove" next Sunday,' enthused Mum. 'So beautiful! It makes me cry every time I hear him sing it.' Dad, who had now reached the middle pages of the famous newspaper and was studying some pictures of young ladies on the beach and an elephant eating ice-cream, said that it made him cry too, and if Alfie was singing 'O for the Wings of a Dove' on Sunday he wasn't going to church.

I liked those people. They groused a lot about their church and they are the interested, reliable ones who are always there.

We reached London after dark, just as some torrential rain was getting well under way and beating a merry tattoo on the station roof. Within seconds we were all being borne along in the surging mass on the platform. My travelling companions were bawling cheerios, a friend who had come to meet me was bawling, 'Over here!', a small child atop a pile of luggage was bawling its head off – and a loud-speaker was bawling something about a train that wasn't there and wasn't likely to be there.

8

Togetherness

My friend Horatio divides his regular churchgoing between two very different churches in the same town. 'I find the difference in atmosphere really invigorating,' he explained. 'At one church the singing by the choir is always serene, uplifting – yes, peerless, but then, sometimes one feels the need to come down to earth a bit and on those Sundays I go to the other church. This one must be unique. The building is late Victorian but I should think the style of service harks back unchanged to eighteenth century hell-fire sermon days. They don't actually have a hell-fire preacher these days although the present vicar is a really gripping actor and gesticulates and shouts a lot and you just don't notice the length of his sermons. It's all very loud and gripping. They've got a big choir and they're always very loud and gripping too.'

'A beautiful, unspoilt Georgian town set around an exquisite medieval parish church in the serene outskirts of the city,' is how the town guide for visitors describes the place where my friend Horatio lives. He proudly agrees with that description, except for the word 'unspoilt'. 'Y'see, it's like this,' he explained, 'this had always been a well connected area – you know, a place of genteel quality, but then, in 1880, they shoved up this red brick monstrosity with a tower like a pepper-pot at the end of the town and called it St Cuthbert's. Luckily, the builders hid most of it behind the Corn Exchange – and nobody ventured behind the Corn Exchange in those days – well, not the kind of people who attended the exquisite parish church, and most people did go there.'

'But if they'd built the new church, I suppose there must have been some people who wanted it,' I suggested.

'Oh, yes,' Horatio confirmed, 'they were the people who actually *lived* behind the Corn Exchange. The new church had a hell-fire preacher and a big congregation right from the start. My great grandfather ran a fish and chip shop next door to the vestry and he was in the choir. Great big powerful men's choir it was – they all knew how to sing. They did it regularly every Saturday night in the 'Prince Blücher'. They didn't have a church organ then but they had a brass band and everything went with a swing.'

'And today,' I said, 'all at St Cuthbert's must feel very fortunate that they still have a large choir.'

'Right,' he agreed, 'and now we have an organ, of course and we've been invaded by ladies who certainly match the men in vigorous enthusiasm and what the vicar calls general boisterous bellowing. We've still got the brass band and that's going great guns – and its conductor is also the organist so everything ties in very well.'

'And now, what about the town church?' I asked, 'the

medieval one that the town guide speaks of with such delight.'

'Ah!' he said, 'as you might expect in a revered historic town like ours (the right side of the Corn Exchange) things are very musically satisfactory. Their choir gives as many recitals as they sing at the church services and they're champions year after year at the big musical festivals. They sing at cathedrals and have made some DVDs that sell very well and keep them in the musical news. They're a top-drawer choir y'see!'

I dared to ask a sensitive question. I said, 'In these days of team ministries and a lot more "togetherness" among the churches, what kind of relationship do these top choir people have with the choir of St Cuthbert's?'

Horatio gazed at me in bewilderment. 'Relationship?' he gasped. 'Relationship! We don't have anything like *that*! Their vicar just downloads onto St Cuthbert's choir any big rowdy wedding services in which his choir are expected to sing stuff from Hollywood musicals or hymn tunes that used to be affectionately referred to as "chucking out time in the Rhonda Valley". Y'see his choir just don't *do* that kind of thing. They are wedded to unaccompanied medieval murmurings in Latin. They don't have anything to do with tunes that people whistle or hum or bawl in the bath. Well, you really can't expect them to belt out things like "The Battle Hymn of the Republic" which seems so popular these days for wedding services where a cheerful musical noise is essential, no matter how inappropriate the words are!'

'So St Cuthbert's choir are often singing in those hallowed, exalted parish church choir stalls,' I said.

'That's right, they perform full blast at the posh place,' he assured. 'Mind you, their vicar always thanks the St Cuthbert's lot profusely and most wedding parties seem to want them to be photographed with the bride and groom and go along to the reception for a drink or two.' Horatio sighed, 'And on those occasions there's never a single sighting of anyone from the top-drawer choir. I think they go away to somewhere peaceful and suffer, thinking of their choir stalls being desecrated by a moronic mob!'

And then, cruelly adding to the strain and anxiety suffered by the parish church choir, there appeared so suddenly the scare of the protesting Victorian sewers. Built to accommodate the demands of a town a quarter the size of the present town, they had coped magnificently with the expansion of the area for over 120 years and had now, at last, protested against modern neglect and incompetence as immediate catastrophic breakdown had threatened right under the parish church. The unavoidable result had been the immediate closure of the whole building and its handing over to a cohort of workmen who, strong rumour had it, ate their lunchtime sandwiches and read scurrilous newspapers in the choir stalls. It was tragic enough having the awful gung-ho St Cuthbert's mob there, bellowing their way through flashy wedding services, but workmen sprawled about the stalls chewing sandwiches and reading scurrilous newspapers – could things get any worse?

Yes, they could. Embracing a carefully nurtured tradition, the work on the sewer exceeded its time limit indefinitely and the parish church congregation found temporary places of worship further afield. One or two members did actually stay locally and ventured behind the Corn Exchange to attend a choral service at St Cuthbert's. Horatio reported that from these encounters two came away with ringing in their ears, two escaped by a side door before the end of the 20-minute sermon and two were so impressed by the sheer volume of musical praise that they joined the choir there and then.

Meanwhile, the choir of the parish church found no nearby church which offered the right acoustics for their peerless performance and they ended up temporarily in a disused railway locomotive shed which possessed near perfect acoustics for medieval murmurings where once magnificent steam locomotives roared and snorted. Belatedly, fate had been less unkind to the parish church choir. They became increasingly attached to the engine shed, as did members of the congregation who dropped in frequently and at all hours to listen to, and be inspired by the ethereal sounds of the choir – who always seemed to be rehearsing. All was beauty and light. But fate can, of course, be thoroughly cruel and fate continued to dog the parish church choir.

The young, very popular mayor and a leading soprano in the local operatic society were to marry and it was to be a big church and civic event. All arrangements for the wedding service having been completed a week before the parish church's sewer troubles, so organizers were now faced with an unthought-of dilemma. The unthinkable had to be thought. The only other Anglican church in the town large enough for the premier event was St Cuthbert's – that place behind the Corn Exchange.

Suddenly the church became the centre of intense religious and civic interest. Horatio reported that members of the parish church congregation and important people from the town hall had been seen sidling unobtrusively behind the Corn Exchange and making for the embarrassing red brick bulk of St Cuthbert's. Most of them hovered and then dived inside, only to reappear quickly looking puzzled or indignant or both. But as the great day approached well-wishers plucked up courage and descended on the church *en bloc* with forests of exotic potted plants and flowers, rolls of red carpet and tins of perfumed polish. A hasty conference decided that as the wedding was being conducted in St Cuthbert's it was St Cuthbert's choir who should lead the service music from their usual choir stalls and the parish church choir could be accommodated far from the madding crowd in the gallery and perform unaccompanied Tudor motets during the comparative quiet of the signing of the registers. St Cuthbert's choir would, of course, lead the singing of 'Jerusalem' and the usual inappropriate hymns which people normally choose for weddings because they know the tunes. At the wedding, the bridegroom's aunt who was 100 years old had insisted that they should sing her favourite hymn 'Through the Night of Doubt and Sorrow' because that's what she had at her wedding. Her father had been at school with the composer of the tune.

Horatio told me that on the great day he just managed to squeeze into the last available sliver of space at the back of St Cuthbert's. 'The whole thing was fantastic,' he enthused. 'It was like the last night of the Proms. There was even clapping when the parish church choir sang their motets – from people with a keen sense of hearing. At the end of the service the happy couple eased their way down the aisle through the massed ranks of friends and photographers (a mounted policeman would have been useful), the St Cuthbert's organist excelled himself with a riotous voluntary that sounded like something played on a steam roundabout organ in a thunderstorm and, waiting in the churchyard, the brass band blasted out the 'Old Comrades' March'.

Prior to the spectacular mayoral wedding the area of the town behind the Corn Exchange was a constant niggling embarrassment to the town council who always endeavoured determinedly to attract and direct the town's thousands of admiring visitors to its superb Georgian centre and glorious medieval parish church and as far away as possible from the blatantly Victorian shambles behind the Corn Exchange. Around St Cuthbert's a number of packed terraces of workmen's cottages trailed, punctuated by some forbidding look-ing empty warehouses, a depot for the town's dustcarts, a glue factory, a small defunct gasworks and a huge fried fish and chips emporium whose beguiling odours generally enveloped the area.

As the wedding party moved regally back into the main town and its most famous hotel, a few hundred out-of-town sightseers found themselves wandering around the environs of St Cuthbert's, many drawn by the enticing aroma of the fish and chips emporium. To a party of young estate agent consultants the place was a revelation and they returned to their firms full of the brightest ideas. Some months later Horatio sent me a beautifully produced glossy local magazine. It contained the usual articles about the beauty of 'this unique Georgian town' but almost half its capacity was taken up with estate agents' articles and advertisements in which the word 'Victorian', once a dirty word in art circles, was used to promote the great attractiveness of 'these delightful, much sought after bijou Victorian residences, some rare opportunities to secure luxury domestic conversions in former prestigious commercial buildings, together with exciting news of forthcoming superb new family homes with ample parking space' (the defunct gasworks site was proving ideal). Even St Cuthbert's was described as 'interesting' and the fish and chips emporium as an 'unusual surviving Victorian community feature'. Most of the advertisements warned, 'Only two left!' and encouraged, 'Fully staffed site office open Sundays' and 'Spend the day in this beautiful town'.

'Isn't it wonderful! The whole town is now becoming one united flourishing entity,' claimed my enthusiastic friend, Horatio, 'and when you think about it, the entire miracle was brought about by good old St Cuthbert's.'

'And what about the two choirs?' I enquired. 'I suppose they are more understanding of each other now, more togetherness – a good relationship.'

'Relationship?' he gasped. 'Relationship! We don't have anything like *that*! Their vicar just downloads onto St Cuthbert's choir any big rowdy wedding services. I seem to have said this somewhere before.'

Some things *don't* change!

9

Indispensable

I arrived at the small English seaside town for a few days' holiday at the close of the season. This, of course, is the best time to arrive at any English seaside town – when all the holiday-makers have returned home swamped and frozen, and the sun bursts forth in all its watery brilliance for the first time in months.

Life around the parish church was comfortably settling back into its well-loved winter routine with the usual large gatherings at the church whist drives and dances, and the usual four people at Sunday Evensong. And this year the church council were settling back to consider a most intriguing question – what to do with the Major-General's lectern. The Major-General had given the lectern in a rash mood many years ago. It was the most hideous creation anyone in the church had ever seen, and only the organist who had been there for 40 years had never seen it, because he never saw anything but choirboys with filthy collars and people who wanted to get married and asked him to play 'Here Comes the Bride' which he didn't like.

The lectern was of solid brass and looked like a sort of large tea-tray shot through with dozens of holes, and fixed on a stand as thick as a tree trunk. This in turn rested on three feet which closely resembled cannon balls. It had been endured for so many years because the Major-General always gave a most generous cheque towards reducing the deficit on the annual church accounts, and always loaned the grounds of the Manor House for the summer fête and sale. This function hadn't enjoyed a single fine day for 21 years, and during that time the Major-General had further endeared himself to everyone by allowing them to fight over the jumble and white elephants in the drier atmosphere of his Regency drawing-room.

But now the fatal blow had fallen. The lady who cleaned the lectern had moved from the parish and no other lady could be found sporting enough to carry on the brave work. So it was generally and thankfully agreed that the time had come when the lectern should be replaced. The vicar was even willing to pay for a new wooden one, but the problem was what to do with the old one and how to break the news to its donor and still retain his support in the matter of annual deficits and washed-out garden fêtes. For although he was a generous man, it was well known that the Major-General would stand no nonsense. However, the vicar felt that he could manage the matter successfully and had promised the church council that he would have 'a quiet little chat' with the Major-General as soon as a suitable opportunity arose. And the church council had backed him to a man and gracefully retired to await the explosion.

The vicar with whom I was staying told me the story as he showed me round the church. He said that during its 400 years it had attracted more than its fair share of gifts. After the lectern, the most unforgettable which he pointed out was a gold and red wooden organ screen, generously carved to represent a lot of large fat cherubs with microscopic wings all lolling about round the organ pipes blowing trumpets. It had been given, before the days of choirboys, by a wealthy and rather credulous bachelor who believed that all children were thinly-disguised angels.

Suddenly, from out of the vestry a man appeared carrying a ladder and a veteran vacuum cleaner. He looked like a retired heavy-weight boxer, and as he passed us and nearly knocked us down, I noticed that he also looked somewhat cross.

'Don't take any notice of his face,' whispered the vicar, 'he always looks like that. He's our verger. An absolute gem of a man. We just couldn't do without him. *He* can do *anything*. He's the only man for miles who knows how to stoke the boiler without filling the church with coke fumes, and if it hadn't been for him we'd have been let in for at least two organ-blowing motors. He keeps the choirboys in order for the organist – frightens the life out of them! – and you should hear him rallying the congregation in their hymns when they get left behind by the choir! He was a town crier at one time, I believe.' The vicar's face glowed with admiration. 'He also knows all about dealing with woodworm in the roof timbers,' he continued incredulously, 'and he's cured the tower clock of stopping at half-past six. Our oldest inhabitant tells me that when he was a boy the tower clock *always* stopped at half-past six.'

The gem of a verger had now ascended the ladder to the organ screen and all normal conversation became impossible as he switched on the vacuum cleaner and ran the hose over the trumpeting cherubs. Dust disappeared as if by magic from their well-nourished bodies – and escaped in a steady stream all over the floor from the back of the cylinder. The vicar noticed my consternation, and when the cleaner was presently switched off, he assured me, 'That's all right! The thing wouldn't work at all when he picked it up at our last jumble sale. He'll clean up the floor with a dustpan and brush when he comes down. It's simply marvellous how he manages. We'd *never* find another like him!'

As if drawn by a great magnet, we were now standing within a few feet of the Major-General's lectern. The vicar gazed at it with a sort of fascinated horror. 'Thank goodness it's going at last,' he said. His voice was awe-filled. 'Can you imagine anything so – so barbaric!'

We hadn't noticed the verger coming down from the organ screen. He loomed head and shoulders above us. For the first time he spoke. 'It's lovely,' he pronounced from somewhere deep inside himself. 'It's a lovely bit of work. I *admire* it!' He glared down at us as he swung the ladder across his shoulder and moved off. 'If *that* goes, I go,' he rumbled. 'It's a lovely bit of work and *I'm* going to look after it from now on.' A trail of dust from the vacuum cleaner followed him into the vestry.

'That's done it!' quavered the vicar.

Several months later I attended a Sunday Matins at the church. It was a fine summer day and brilliant shafts of sunlight filled the nave. And there, in the brightest spot, gleaming, hideous and unconquered, stood the Major-General's lectern. The vicar had not, after all, had his quiet little chat with the Major-General. The verger had had one with the vicar.

The verger is still indispensable. And so, of course, is the lectern.

10

The Editor's Decision

I have a literary friend who collects parish magazines. He's got thousands of them stacked in a little room at the top of his house which his wife calls the Chamber of Horrors.

He estimates that, apart from over 10,000 vicars' letters which keep on talking about Dear Parishioners, making renewed efforts and going forward together, and serial stories which last for twenty years at a page a month, they also contain close on 40,000 advertisements about undertakers who are experts in arranging dignified last journeys at rock-bottom prices, and butchers who seem to have inexhaustible supplies of home-killed pork and sausages containing no preservatives.

Whenever my literary friend is in the vicinity of a strange church – and he's come across some very strange ones in his time – he always goes in and tries to obtain a copy of the parish magazine for his collection. I was with him recently on a walking tour in the West of England, when we came upon a delightful neo-Gothic nightmare. It stood next door to a twin nightmare which appeared to be a brush factory, and the only way you could tell the difference between the church and the brush factory was to read the notices outside their respective doors. One invited you to do your duty by coming to church and supporting the free-will offering scheme, and the other one invited you to take a job where experience wasn't necessary, wages were fantastic, and everyone got free lunches.

Resisting the temptation of this earthly paradise, we pushed open the large church door which was covered with dozens of rusty drawing pins, two hopelessly out-of-date notices announcing superior jumble sales, and a threatening message from the vicar to the effect that unless some people did something soon about tidying up their family graves they (the graves, not the people) would be levelled off. There was also a venerable curling notice signed by a much earlier vicar which said simply, 'Dogs are not allowed in this Church.'

My literary friend was in luck. Numerous memorial windows full of great thick pieces of blue and red glass, including one which, for some reason, depicted a gentleman in chain mail playing a harp, successfully blotted out most of the daylight, but an electric light burned above the bookstand. Obviously the enthusiasm in this church centred round the bookstand. This was a long, battered dining table which stood at the back of the church below an enormous monument to a local nineteenth-century banker who, apparently, had been pious, upright, liberal, compassionate and loved by all, and had bequeathed a seat to the churchyard with his name carved right across the back in letters six inches high.

On a large piece of cardboard at the back of the

bookstand, someone had run amok with a brush and a liberal supply of red paint. 'Have you seen this?' blazed the brush marks, in a gloriously unconventional mixture of script and block capitals, and an arrow snaked down to a spot on the table where, I suppose, a special book or pamphlet should have lain. Perhaps someone had taken it, because it wasn't there, and in its place was a very loud check cap with a villainous-looking bent peak, on which was pinned a piece of paper inscribed 'Left in the back pew last Sunday evening.'

Another arrow, which started off as a thin red line and ended up as a large fat smudge, pointed to a pile of parish magazines on which was a postcard inviting you to 'Please take one. Price 50p or more.' There was a great deal more literature on the dining table-cum-bookstand, including a display of books which were so cleverly and delicately arranged that, if you picked one up to look at it, the rest fell all over the floor and knocked down a vase of dead daffodils and a tottering pile of two or three hymn books with no covers.

But it was, of course, the magazines which drew my literary friend like a magnet. So engrossed was he that he didn't notice someone who had materialized from the blue and red encircling gloom. He was a small, bird-like character, enveloped in a sort of sad black gown which dragged behind him like a rather neglected train, and distinguished him as the verger.

'Magazine money goes in there,' he rasped, indicating a cocoa tin with a slit in the lid. 'Not that the magazine's worth 50p,' he went on, pushing himself under my friend's arm and snatching away the copy he had been studying. He flicked the pages over, and pointed to the vicar's letter.

'I meantersay,' he appealed to us, "oo wants to read that stuff? 'E's bad enough with 'is sermons without 'aving to read it all over again in 'is letters. What they want in this magazine is letters like they 'ave in our local paper.' A sudden enthusiasm seemed to grip him. He fumbled violently among the generous yards of his gown, and presently drew out a roll of dog-eared paper completely covered with large, thick writing. He thrust it eagerly at my literary friend. "Ere's a letter I've written,' he said. 'I've offered it to the magazine editor dozens of times. I've told 'im it would really stir things up if a few *vital* things like this was put in the magazine.'

He was doubtless right. With a total absence of full stops and commas for over three and a half pages, he had stated in an extraordinarily firm and down-to-earth manner what he would do with the choirboys, the local bus company, the bell-ringers and the government, and had concluded with the stirring call, 'Church of England move with the times or perish is what I say signed Furious.'

'I mean, it's what people *want*, isn't it?' he threatened my literary friend. He turned on me and handed me a copy of the magazine without even asking for the 50p. 'You just look at *that*!' He pointed to the obituary column, printed below an advertisement for wedding dresses on easy payments. "Oo wants to read about people dying and 'ow old they were? Look at this one – ninety-eight and worked in the Post Office for fifty years.' He was momentarily without speech.

A second more, and I'm sure he would have recovered and made some telling comment on the gentleman listed immediately below the Post Office worker. He had been only 90, but had ended up with 33 grandchildren after working for the Gas Company from his youth, tirelessly cleaning street lamps until the very last one had been converted to electricity.

But the verger had lost his chance. There was a clatter at the door, and a large, superior-looking cleric rolled in towards us. 'Ah! Willie!' he boomed at the verger, and the sound was tremendous in that cavernous place. 'The coke is arriving! At last the coke is arriving! Nip round to the back and see it in, and when you have done that I want you to . . .' Willie dissolved without a word.

My literary friend was lost in his magazine. The large, superior-looking cleric concentrated all his attention on him and ignored me completely. (Large, superior-looking clerics *do* seem to ignore me completely.) 'I'm the vicar,' he introduced himself. 'I see you *are* interested in our little literary effort. Well, we *do try* to *raise* the standard of the parish magazine and I think we *succeed*. In so *many* parishes the magazine is *pathetic* . . . a disgrace . . .'

He started shepherding my literary friend up the aisle in an extraordinarily bulldozer-like manner. 'Come up to the vestry,' he demanded. 'Let me show you the sort of thing they were calling a magazine when I arrived here.' My literary friend was keen. The vicar was keen. They didn't notice me. I made to pick up a book from the cleverly and delicately arranged display. As it collapsed, I tried to save the vase of dead daffodils. But it was no good. They were swept to the floor. And, as the last hymn book fell it broke the vase to smithereens.

11

Boniface

My friend Boniface comes from a musical family. His great-uncle used to play the piano accompaniment to cowboy films in the silent era at one of the first electric Kinemas. A cousin could play the entire 'William Tell' overture on the mouth organ before he was three years old, another cousin could play the harp with his toes, and Boniface himself was named after a much-revered family dog who went into ecstasies and rolled all over the place whenever he heard the local brass band playing 'Colonel Bogey'.

And nowadays Boniface is the organist and choirmaster at an incredibly ancient pile in flattest Suffolk. He has strong beliefs and reckons that the average modern vicar moves into a parish, upsets the choir and, when the choir has almost disappeared, moves on to another parish and does the same thing there. Boniface says that's why so many churches have such abysmal choirs, or no choirs at all.

But Boniface's choir have a glorious unassailable confidence that no vicar will ever succeed in making them disappear. Boniface's large, rosy, 'favourite-uncle' exterior houses a will of iron which has enabled him, among other things, to establish a tradition that his favourite hymn, 'Christian, dost thou see them?' is sung on every possible occasion throughout the church's year, including Christmas Day. A former vicar did once suggest to him that the hymn was really only meant for Passiontide but, as Boniface told him in no uncertain terms, you couldn't keep a good tune down with silly arguments like that.

The new vicar in Boniface's parish is, however, a rare exception. He's a very learned, middle-aged, jolly bachelor who flatters Boniface and the choir no end and never questions their tradition of singing only solidly Victorian music. Indeed he insists on singing everything with them in a huge, flat, tuneless growl. Sometimes he upsets the musical balance a bit in the softer passages of some anthems and settings, but this is only very seldom because Boniface's choir don't go in much for softer passages.

All the choir appreciate the new vicar. He is very keen on holding special commemoration services and thanksgivings and reunion services, all of which call for quantities of noisy music and are followed by a great binge in the village hall. Quite early on he discovered that many ladies in the congregation were superb cooks who were ever ready and eager to display their skills at parish gatherings so, as with the choir, he has encouraged them by increasing the number of special services entailing lavish refreshments.

The choirmen's forte outside their church singing is barber-shop singing and, as soon as he heard them, the new vicar realized to his immense delight and excitement that he was a born barber-shop singer, and he joined them on the spot. The choirmen find his growl a little awkward to camouflage, but the situation affords great advantages. Relations between the vicar and the choir are now so idyllic that Boniface can choose the noisiest of the most outrageously sentimental hymns and anthems and 'old favourites' of all kinds for the Sunday services with the vicar's blessing, and therefore without fear of any effective opposition from the handful of the congregation who believe that Christian worship can only be truly expressed in unaccompanied plainchant and melodies from early English manuscripts.

Not that this small dissident band are unduly discouraged by the recent course of events. During services they are always to be seen dotted about the congregation making their silent protest about Boniface's atrocious choice of music. Their protest consists in displaying prominently a tightly-closed hymn book and equally tightly-closed lips and staring fixedly ahead during the singing of all hymns unacceptable to them. Boniface says it must be quite a strain for them to protest in this way, seeing that they only like things early English, because when they stare ahead they are confronted not only with the choir but with the east window, which is barely 150 years old and is full of the most belligerent, ugly-faced, red and blue glass saints and war-like characters in Boer War uniforms astride what look like charging brewery dray horses.

But until a few months ago, as far as the choir and most of the congregation were concerned, everything was proceeding very happily and looked set fair to remain so as long as the vicar remained such an enthusiastic member of the barber-shop singers.

Alas, life seldom stays so perfect. In the cloudless summer skies over Boniface's church, an annoying little cloud suddenly appeared in the shape of a new curate. I heard the disturbing story as soon as I arrived at the church to join the choir for Sunday Matins at the start of a short holiday I was spending with Boniface. 'The new vicar's great,' explained Boniface, 'no trouble at all. He knows what we like and we all get along fine. But this new curate – I'm telling you, he needs some watching.'

'What's his trouble?' I asked.

'He's got hold of a new hymn book,' explained Boniface darkly. 'He wants us to use it. He says the tunes are nearly all based on early English music and are very simple and beautiful and we'll all grow to love them. He says we'll be thrilled.'

'What's going to be done about this book?' I asked.

'The choir won't touch it, of course,' vowed Boniface, 'especially as two of us have just finished a month's work renovating all our old *Ancient and Moderns*.'

'So that's that?' I ventured.

'Ah, but this new curate is crafty,' said Boniface. 'He keeps on suggesting holding a little exploratory meeting to discuss the church music.'

'Very democratic,' I said.

'Very cunning,' corrected Boniface.

Apparently, what the new curate had in mind was a cosy wine-and-cheese party where he could meet the choir and show them the new book – 'such a tastefully bound little volume, so nice to handle' – and play over one or two of its beautiful, simple hymns after which he was sure they would all agree that this was for them. By the time we'd processed into the chancel for Matins it was evident that news of the curate's plan for introducing his early English treasure had reached every nook and cranny of the parish. From the choir stalls I saw a huddled mass of indignant faces (the pews are very narrow and close together), punctuated sparsely by faces alight with pure joy. The early English camp was scenting victory.

We started the service in dashing style with 'Stand up, Stand up for Jesus' and we roared through it even more heartily than usual, I thought, but now even that normally shattering experience could not touch the jubilant opposition as Boniface's familiar choice of music ran its thunderous course.

In the vestry after the service the vicar, as usual, started to enthuse about the next barber-shop programme. No one was interested. Perhaps he had a sudden horrible vision of life with absolutely no barber-shop singing. He was seen to hurry across the vestry to where a much larger than life contralto towered threateningly over the new curate as he attempted to demonstrate to her the beauties of the new hymn book.

'Ah, the new hymn book!' beamed the vicar. 'As a matter of fact I wanted a word . . .' The large contralto obviously had no intention of moving off, so the vicar carried on. He said how very much he appreciated the new curate's thoroughgoing interest in the music, particularly his suggestion about the new hymn book. Nevertheless, one had to consider . . . He said how interested he had been in the new curate's ideas about an informal, meaningful, family get-together service with meaningful hymns to replace Matins. Nevertheless, one had to consider . . .

To a churchwarden, a great friend of Boniface's, the vicar was later more explicit. He said he really couldn't risk upsetting the choir. After all they were such an integral indispensable part of the parish – always totally dependable, always there when they were wanted and even when they were not wanted. And he could not overlook the fact that it was mainly the members of the choir who did such priceless work in the monumental task of keeping the acres of Victorian graveyard in pristine order, and ensuring that the church's historic heating system displayed some signs of working, and making sure that the roof didn't fall in and that the choir surplices were washed regularly enough to make them look presentable at a distance. After all, what was the routine annoyance of having your favourite early English hymn rejected by the choir, or your efforts to introduce a real family get-together service in place of Matins utterly frustrated, compared with the huge embarrassment and inconvenience of a creeping jungle in the graveyard, a stone cold church with a collapsed roof and two dozen filthy surplices on Christmas Day? One had to be realistic.

Things go on much the same as ever in Boniface's parish and the barber-shop singers go from strength to strength. Recently, quite unexpectedly, the new curate joined them. He says he has some ideas . . .

12

Where Fools Rush In

Traditionally, church choirs attract a variety of unusual characters – members who often upset the new, forward-thinking vicar no end by not immediately loyally falling in with his vigorous, visionary efforts to drag musical Christian praise from the nineteenth century into the twenty-first century in a couple of months. The choir are apt to realize that the vicar, although keen, is tragically short of any kind of musical knowledge and doesn't know what he or she is talking about, or that the vicar has realized that they, the choir, are tragically short of any kind of musical knowledge and don't know what *they* are talking about. So life in such choirs is never dull.

The small-town church choir where my friend Peter is the only surviving male alto is one such case. Peter says you've got to be always on the alert. You never know what the vicar's next move will be – proposing that the choir should abandon their choir stalls and robes and spread themselves among the congregation . . . that they should ditch their hymn books and embrace the vicar's lovely new song book with jolly pop tunes. All for the advancement of the vicar's vital aim of a parish of joyful togetherness. 'You've got to be ready to do battle at any moment,' warns Peter. 'Our choir have the usual unusual characters,' he says, 'but we have one who is a real star turn among star turns. He doesn't agree with the vicar *or* the choir.'

Oscar is a wiry, wild-haired choirman of uncertain age who erupts into the vestry a few minutes before each service and immediately starts expressing his controversial views most urgently on everything to everybody, no matter whether they are listening to him or talking to each other or pretending he's not there. His voice is loud and authoritative and if you do try to listen and get an idea of what he is fuming about you are liable to become as confused as he sounds. The other trouble is that the organist also talks as wildly and loudly and at the same time as Oscar, generally arguing on some subject about which both obviously know absolutely nothing. When the time for the service duly arrives someone in the choir gently reminds the vicar who, apparently oblivious of time, Oscar, the organist and the choir, is generally practising his sermon and gestures before the vestry mirror. The vicar thereupon cuts off Oscar's and the organist's battle of words on inflaming topics like why the railways are in such a mess and who was Jack the Ripper and with a quickly mumbled vestry prayer, herds the choir before him into the choir stalls.

Since I had last been a guest in Peter's church choir, both Oscar and the forward looking vicar had arrived in the parish, so my next visit promised to be quite intriguing according to Peter who delighted in keeping me in touch with events with long, misspelt letters and even longer misspelt e-mails peppered with double and treble exclamation marks to emphasize how much I will be intrigued.

On the Sunday morning of my latest visit Peter and I arrived in the vestry just as the organist was shouting, above the confused babble of choristers' conversation and guffaws, that there was just time before the service to run through the anthem which they'd made such an almighty hash of at the Friday night rehearsal. Nobody appeared to be taking the slightest notice of him and in the midst of the melee Oscar was explaining explosively to the backs of three choirladies that when he was a boy women knew their place in the choir and were allowed to sing only soprano. None of them were allowed to sing contralto because there were five male altos in the choir and no one wanted to hear their voices muddied by women. Peter heaved out of the way a group of choir-boys who were investigating a personal stereo that was apparently refusing to add to the hubbub and grabbed a cassock and surplice for me from the dark place under the organ reserved for robes and anything else that was in the way of the occasional hoover.

Peter dragged the robes through the seemingly immovable groups of gossiping choristers and rather adroitly forged a place for us between the vestry table and a jutting piece of wall sporting an enormous sepia photograph of a grim Victorian former vicar who regarded us with a sort of icy contempt. 'Lucky to get these things for you,' puffed Peter. 'Everybody in the choir has turned up today, the rumour is that the vicar is going to treat us to one of his "going forward in joyful togetherness" proposals in the sermon and that means having a go at the choir.'

'Y'see,' explained a huge bass gentleman who was pushing past us and looked remarkably like the sepia Victorian vicar, 'he thinks it unfriendly of the choir to sit up in the chancel on our own. He says you can't have joyful fellowship with the congregation when you are up there.' He frowned fiercely, 'but you can take this togetherness thing too far. You know, I often think this coming home from the office on the tube each night when there's so much togetherness that we can't move and there's even no room to fall down for those who faint in the heat.' He reached across us to the peg whereon his cassock and surplice were wont to hang. 'Blimey! Someone's pinched it,' he growled. 'It's all the vicar's joyful togetherness that's to blame. What's he think he's doing?'

Peter said to me, 'There he is, the vicar – the one in the pink shirt and the jeans waving his arms about and beaming at himself in front of the mirror. He's going through his sermon. When he starts bundling himself into his cassock and surplice and plastic collar that means that we trail off into church and start the service.' And having finished his mirror sermon with a dramatic flourish that is what the vicar did.

It happens with exciting regularity that when I visit friends' choirs I invariably find myself, during the service, sitting next to the choir's most endearing or thoroughly annoying 'character' and this time in continuing custom it was wild Oscar who became my neighbour as we processed into the choir stalls and he trod heavily on my feet, shuffled his music into instant chaos and, as we started singing the first hymn, informed me in a town crier's voice that the tune was utter piffle and he could have composed a better one in his head in two minutes. He continued to expand on this claim after the hymn had finished, only in rather louder tones, until a soprano in the stall in front of us, a girl who possessed a glorious voice and had the genteel appearance of a cultured English rose, turned round and hissed at him, 'Shut up, you moron!'

Oscar didn't appear to be in the least annoyed at this rebuff. I suppose he was used to that kind of thing but he did now devote himself to the singing until we came to the sermon. Normally, in the manner of choirs, few members listened to the sermon, that was the congregation's responsibility. After all, the congregation didn't do much else in the service – they never seemed to sing and they missed most of the responses. But this was the vital sermon when the vicar was to put forward his ideas for advancing the vital joyful togetherness plans and the choir were naturally suspicious of what it all meant for them.

Certainly those suspicions about the vicar's inspired plans proved to be very well founded. Throughout his sermon his shining enthusiasm for bringing the choir into full joyful togetherness with the congregation by bringing them down out of the choir stalls, minus their old-fashioned robes, right there among the congregation, stirred even those members of the congregation who sat secluded in personal pews, behind pillars and choir members who solved Sunday crosswords during the sermon and the bubbling euphoria brought about by the vicar's joyful togetherness words reached their peak at the end of the service when everyone lined up to shake hands with him in the church porch (except those members who wanted to get the Sunday lunch moving, who slipped out of a side door). Such was his charm that those who thought they agreed with his sermon and those who thought they didn't and those who didn't understand what he was talking about, all gave him the same beaming smile and congratulations, on an inspiring sermon. Some members were even observed joining the back of the queue again in order to shake hands with him a second time and emphasize their delight in him and his exciting ideas for fearlessly going modern and bringing the choir down a peg or two.

For the congregation all this euphoria lasted till just after Sunday lunch when most of them fell asleep and others started to settle back comfortably, mentally confirming their various ingrained parish attitudes, and things were back to normal in no time.

For the choir, however, the threat of their removal from the choir stalls and choir attire to be swallowed up by the congregation remained horribly real. They knew it only needed another joyful togetherness sermon to bring back the enthusiasm for the new vicar's tempting vision of a parish utopia where the choir would no longer lounge in the choir stalls and subject the congregation to long stretches of Latin dirges without even the assistance of surtitles like they had in opera houses. It could be the end of an era.

A few weeks later my friend Peter, the lone alto,

phoned me with the news of the final act (for the time being) at the parochial church council meeting following the famous sermon. The vicar duly opened proceedings with his words of togetherness magic and the council were ready to vote for the new order *en bloc*. But then, at the crucial moment of decision Oscar rose to speak as he did every Sunday in the choir vestry. Oscar was very much on form. He said he warmly welcomed the idea of the choir going down from the choir stalls and singing with the congregation in joyful togetherness, but the whole thing must be *right*. Half a dozen members of the congregation must be assigned to sit with each member of the choir to listen and learn and be instructed throughout the service on how to hold themselves and their hymn books, how to breathe and sing the psalms and hymns with feeling and under-standing. Further, they would be expected to attend choir practice regularly so that their musical progress could be monitored.

'You're getting all this?' Peter asked over the phone.

'Carry on,' I urged.

'Well as you know,' he continued, 'there's one thing our congregation never do at our church, they never sing. They never have done. They open their hymn books at the right place and then concentrate on listen-ing to see if the choir get into difficulties so that they can complain to the vicar after the service. Everyone likes having a go at the choir – it's a sort of revered trad-ition and despite even the joyous influence of new-age vicars, there were revered traditions that remained . . . Anyway, Oscar went on and on for hours and no one seemed able to shut him up – until finally when he had entirely lost the thread of what he was saying and got on to a subject that had nothing to do with where the choir sat, the vicar managed hastily to bring the meeting to a close with a brief snappy prayer about togetherness and we all went on our separate ways home at about one o'clock in the morning.'

The choir really warmed to Oscar. Peter tells me that no one in the parish – not even the vicar – talks about bringing the choir down into the congregation these days. Oscar himself doesn't understand why. He fumes, 'People go over the top about their radical new ideas for the Church's future – then they get cold feet and forget about everything. Pathetic lot!'

13

A Matter of Faith

One fine Saturday afternoon while on a summer cycling holiday in the West Country I'd met this village vicar, a jovial Humpty-Dumpty character, as I wandered around admiring his homely Victorian church. Presently we got to talking about church music and those who performed it and within minutes he'd invited me to help out in the choir the next day. 'Half of them are away on holiday at the moment,' he explained, 'and the other half so miss them they are all over the place even in the hymns they know. You'd be very welcome.'

I thanked him and assured him I'd be delighted. 'Every little helps,' I said.

'Splendid! Great! Wonderful!' he exclaimed excitedly, as vicars are apt to exclaim excitedly these days on the rare occasions when someone is persuaded to join the shrinking choir.

'Is the choirmaster on holiday?' I asked.

'Oh, no,' the vicar said soberly. 'He never goes on holiday – he never lets up on the choir. It's almost as if he thinks they'll disappear if he's away. He's a perfectionist, you see. He can detect the slightest imperfection when the choir are singing and even in the middle of a service he will point to an offender and scowl in a most unsettling manner.' The vicar glanced around almost furtively in the empty church where we stood. 'He points at me sometimes. It puts me right off, you know.'

'There are some very disturbing choirmasters about,' I sympathized.

'But at least I don't feel singled out,' he continued. 'Knowing our choir, he's pointing at people all over the place right through the service. The choir are used to it, of course, and it doesn't worry them. They never take any notice anyway.'

In the choir vestry on Sunday morning I was made very welcome by the holiday-depleted choir who told me all about themselves and asked all about me in a matter of minutes – and met another visiting choirman introduced as Hooter Harold, an alto who had been in the choir some years before moving to London. 'That was in the days when it was usual to have male altos in the choir – before all these contralto women took over,' growled a very obvious bass called Big Fred.

'Strange how contraltos always seem to be sort of battle-axe types,' mused a tenor gentleman whose wife and daughter sang soprano in the choir.

'That's only in stories and plays,' put in the organist struggling into a veteran crumpled cassock with rolled up sleeves, 'and in comic opera, of course, there's that wonderful woman in *The Mikado* – Natisha . . .'

'You don't have to go to comic opera to find 'em,' said the tenor. 'They started here years ago, caused no end of trouble. What about Fiona Cuttlethorpe for instance.'

'I thought she turned into a bass,' said Hooter Harold.

'Only when she had a cold,' amended the tenor, 'or when Big Fred was away on one of his darts tournament tours.'

Then all discussion ceased abruptly as the choirmaster marched into the vestry and immediately commanded, 'Attention choir!' He was an endlessly tall, bony man of uncertain age with narrow, sharp features and sparse prickly grey hair. He stood to attention by the piano. 'The anthem did not go well at practice on Friday,' he stated, ' it was in fact abysmal. It must be correct this morning, it must be nothing less than immaculate, perfect. For you to achieve this I must *insist* that you all watch me the *whole* time you are singing.' And he went on and on.

I whispered to the tenor, 'I don't know this anthem. I've never seen it before. I *must* look at the music while we're singing, I can't watch him all the time.'

'It doesn't matter about that,' assured the tenor, 'everybody will be looking at their music or anywhere but at him, they always do. Y'see, when he conducts he develops these awful grimaces – quite demonic really – and turns a sort of red purple in the face, awful to behold. He'll be pointing all over the place at everyone. Pointing helps him. He wouldn't know what to do with his hands otherwise.'

'I really don't know what to do about this,' I said.

'Just sing,' the tenor grinned encouragingly. 'It'll sound all right down in the congregation – that's what really matters. Down there they think anything's all right as long as the choir sings it and they don't have to.

They appreciate us. They always give most generously to our summer outing fund – they really like us.'

'It doesn't sound as though your choirmaster likes you lot very much,' I ventured.

'Oh, no,' he agreed, 'he doesn't like us. He never stands any of us a drink even at Christmas and if he meets us in the street when he's with his wife he looks annoyed and she kind of looks through us in a pained sort of way. She doesn't come to church but I think she's heard all about us. But we're vitally important to him, y'see – he looks on us as a challenge and the choir have *never* taken any notice of what he says.'

'True,' agreed the tenor, 'that's why we're such a challenge. He revels in big challenges.'

I imagine we were indeed a really exciting challenge to him during the service. Whenever we were singing he was jabbing at all of us in lightning succession and, on more than one occasion, with both hands simultaneously, but the choir with years of experience, I suppose, managed superbly to avoid eye contact with him and automatically took their timing from Big Fred whose steam-roller pace was so loudly imposed that we couldn't do much else. So we got through the hymns and psalms in a ponderous, dignified manner at half the speed indicated by the choirmaster's flaying fingers and distorted features. Seemingly oblivious of the situation he proceeded until we reached the musical highlight of the service, the aforementioned anthem which I did not know. I enjoyed it nevertheless. It was one of those boisterous efforts turned out by the dozen by Victorian church musicians the singing of which always makes my day. They also endear themselves to one for another reason. I'm ever fascinated by the evidence that so many Victorian composers chose to set to music some of the most incomprehensible, bloodthirsty passages in the Old Testament. The old favourite we now sang was no exception and we performed it with all the enthusiasm and power of a champion brass band blasting through a rattling good military march.

When we finished and sat down rather breathlessly and the choirmaster had mopped his face and returned it to a normal expression, the tenor, next to me, whispered that there would be a short silence now so that everyone could meditate on the words of the anthem. It was the vicar's idea, he explained, and the plan was that people could discuss their reactions over coffee after the service. He said that no one ever actually did this, however, because the words of the anthem were always so chopped up by the music that no one in the congregation could piece them together to make any kind of sense of them and the choir only thought about the tune and seldom knew what the anthem was about. But the idea pleased the vicar because he'd thought of it and it kept him in a good mood, so everyone was happy.

After the service, as I lingered in the coffee room with the small group of choristers who had not escaped immediately to The Goat and Compasses, the choirmaster approached me with measured step and solemn mien. 'Tell me,' he asked, 'what were you endeavouring to sing in the anthem? Was it alto or tenor – or were you attracted to the bass line?' I laughed dutifully at his pointed remarks as you are supposed to laugh when dealing with choirmasters who make pointed remarks. I always remember the words of a very old, very experienced choirman who told me that if people wanted to enjoy being in the church choir it was essential that they never allowed themselves to become upset because the choirmaster hurled derogatory remarks at them regularly throughout entire choir rehearsals. He explained that choirmasters were artists and had artistic temperaments that could be seriously hurt when choir members got rebellious and failed to appreciate the outpourings of brilliant humour so generously offered at every choir practice.

The choirmaster seemed pleased at my reaction to his enquiry about my singing ability and looked as though he was about to linger with our group, whereupon the group gently and politely dissolved leaving me with the choirmaster who was already deep into his cherished plans for making the choir the finest in England. He said they were the same plans, unaltered, that he'd had since he was appointed 20 years ago and his faith in them had carried him through to the present day when the choir still hadn't changed a bit. But the vital point was that he had faith that he would eventually transform them. He really did believe that he could make a silk purse out of a pig's ear. All the pigs had to do was to watch him for every moment that he conducted and their performances would become pure perfection – as finest silk.

I thought a lot about that village choir and their choirmaster as I cycled away on my tour. Theirs was a happy lot. The choir *enjoyed* the way they sang, unchanged over the years and – if they ever realized it – had simple faith that they would surely continue in their enjoyable tradition. The choirmaster was dauntless in his pioneering faith that in the fullness of time he would surely redeem them from their misguided ways. All were happy in their faith. Faith was the answer.

14

A Tailless Tale

It all started with the new rector's Manx cat, Chunky.

The lady with the commanding voice and pink hair who had occupied the front pew below the pulpit for 40 years and ran everything and everybody in the parish, said that the new rector's Manx cat frightened her Alsatian. A friend mildly suggested that it seemed perhaps a little odd that a small cat who even lacked a tail should be capable of frightening an outsized Alsatian, but the lady had retorted that it was obviously *because* the cat had no tail that he frightened her darling Twinkle. She said that Twinkle was *always* frightened of things he didn't understand. And who could understand a Manx cat? After all, no one seemed to know why they hadn't got tails.

It appeared that the mysterious Chunky was the only character in the village whom Twinkle didn't understand. He was afraid of no one else. He had fearlessly bitten the postman at least half a dozen times and commanded the greatest respect from the tradesmen and the paper-boy. Indeed, the paper-boy had for years hurled the papers at the lady's front door from the safety of the other side of the gate, and for years Twinkle had expertly torn them to shreds.

I met Twinkle's owner quite by accident in the Lilliputian village restaurant where I was lunching before keeping an appointment with the rector. As she made to sit at my table, her shopping bag swept my bowl of soup neatly into my lap. I assured her that I was quite all right, and, as so often happens in such cases, we continued talking. When she learned that I was a visitor who hoped to attend one or two of the services at the church she became extremely interested and I didn't have to say another word for at least 20 minutes. It was only necessary for me to nod and smile dutifully on the rare occasions when she stopped for breath, and I was able to get on with my lunch quite well.

I had apparently arrived on the scene at a most unfortunate time. The new rector appeared to be a most unco-operative – indeed, downright unfriendly – man. The lady had been willing to guide him and initiate him into the whole set-up of the parish, but what thanks, what appreciation did she get? He completely ignored her and her plans for the parish, and even more regrettable, his un-Christian attitude was now having a most deplorable effect on some of the more unstable members of the church council who were also beginning to step out of line and speak up for themselves. After all the years she had so unstintingly devoted to guiding them the lady felt their attitude to be most ungrateful. And it was entirely the fault of the new rector.

Now the *old* rector had been quite different. Such a *dear* man! Everything was so friendly with him. During the sermon he would lean *right* over the edge of the pulpit and talk down to you as if you were all in a cosy informal little group in someone's drawing room. Many were the times that she had retrieved his sermon notes as they had slid over the edge and fluttered down forgotten over the front pews. Once she had narrowly escaped being brained by a falling *Ancient & Modern*. 'Everything was so *intimate* in those days,' she boomed, 'but now the new man stands up there mumbling to no one in particular like a faulty radio set.' And of course, to make matters worse there was his Manx cat. The old rector had a cat – a proper one with a tail – and Twinkle had spent many happy hours chasing it from one end of the village to the other. But the Manx monstrosity wasn't a nice type at all. He simply refused to be chased and just sat there bristling in a most bad-tempered way.

For a moment, for some unfathomable reason, the lady halted, and having finished my meal I rose quickly and excused myself. As I left the cash desk the commanding voice rose again and filled the restaurant. 'Don't take any notice if the rector is rude to you. It's his *way*. One must try to be charitable . . .'

The rector received me with old-world courtesy in the barn-like spaciousness of the old-world rectory. The grand staircase was devoid of carpet or linoleum and on the half-landing were two stuffed elephants' feet overlooked by a glass case containing the moth-eaten remains of a vulture. A strip of disintegrating coconut matting led across the hall floorboards to the study.

It was pleasant to find that the rector appeared a mild, delightfully vague, middle-aged type, far removed from the ecclesiastical despot of the lady's description. He invited me to sit down, and as soon as he realized that there was nowhere to sit, very kindly removed the coal-scuttle, a bunch of bananas and three bound volumes of *Punch* from a one-armed rocking chair, and made me most comfortable. He then asked how he could help me, and on being informed that we had corresponded and he had invited me to call, he said, 'Of course,' and started sorting through the tottering wads of paper on his desk to find my letter. Eventually he discovered it on the floor where, he explained, he put everything he didn't want to forget. When he had scanned it he beamed and said they'd be delighted to see me in the congregation during my holiday in the village. He wondered if I'd like to act as sidesman. He'd speak to the churchwarden, Mr Black – sorry Mr Smith, who had the rota. Or had he already done so? Never mind, I'd be very welcome.

Suddenly a pile of the papers behind the rector's typewriter toppled to the floor and there rose to view a small tabby cat. He composed himself primly and sat gazing at me, a chubby, tailless creature of infinite fascination. This I knew must be Chunky, vanquisher of Twinkle.

Then, before the rector could introduce us, a loud knocking sounded at the front door. He ambled off murmuring apologies and returned a few moments later carrying my plastic mac. 'How very nice of her,' he beamed. 'That was a member of our church council, a Mrs — er —. She said she met you in the restaurant just now and you left your mac behind. She was taking her dog for a walk and thought she'd drop it in.' Puzzlement mingled with his beaming smile. 'Until now I haven't been able to get to know her at all. I've called on her a number of times and got no reply, and she's always left the church before I can get down to the west door after evensong. Of course, I see her at the church council meetings, but for some reason she always seems to be so cross then . . . but this is wonderful. She's *never* called at the rectory. She's broken the ice at last! How nice!'

I hadn't noticed that Chunky had left us until I spotted him through the study window. He was streaking across the wilderness of the rector's back garden as only a Manx cat can streak. And ahead of him, running for his life, was an outsized Alsatian dog.

'Yes, I *know* things are going to be a lot happier from now on,' the rector was enthusing. He had his back to the window. He didn't see the face of the Alsatian's owner as it appeared over the garden fence. I said nothing.

15

Ye Choirs of New Jerusalem

Until a year or so ago, my old friend George always kept very quiet about the South of England town where he lived and acted as organist at the parish church. He maintained that he didn't exactly *hate* the town, but if he thought about it for long it made him so depressed that life was hardly worth living. Few of his fellow townsfolk seemed to like the place either. They didn't even like each other. At meeting after meeting of the town council there were tremendous rows, which raged till the early hours, and which were a veritable godsend to the local newspaper which never had anything else to report. They were also very successful in the encouraging of whole pages of vitriolic letters from people who attacked the council, the refuse carts, the vicar, dogs in food shops, and each other with unabated fury for weeks on end. The editor would then insert a little notice stating 'This correspondence is now closed', and someone would immediately stir up something else.

But a great change came. There arose in that town a brand-new concrete and glass multi-storied office block. It belonged to the Government, and was very important. It contained scores of offices, all of which blazed with electric light all day and half the night, whether they were in use or not. Wherever you went in the town, the new building loomed over you. It was the biggest blot on the landscape for miles, and was secretly envied by every neighbouring town. And in the place of its birth, it worked a miracle, for it cemented the townsfolk into one proud happy community.

George was particularly proud and happy, because the Government department which employed him, and had previously been housed in a condemned work-house, was transferred to the tenth floor of the new block. He had more than once invited me to 'drop up' and see him there.

So, finding myself in the vicinity late one autumn afternoon, I decided to take him at his word. A lift hurtled me up to the appropriate floor where, in an outer office in the film-studio brilliance of dozens of lights, I came upon a very smart, business-like young lady, who sat behind a beautiful desk polishing her nails.

I introduced myself, and asked if I might see George. I said that I hoped I wasn't disturbing him at a busy time. At this the young lady looked rather taken aback and said, 'Good gracious, no, there's never any trouble about *that.*' Then she put away her nail polish into a handbag as big as a travelling trunk, and kindly announced me.

In an inner office of boardroom proportions, my friend sat in splendid isolation on the edge of a most impressive desk. He held a somewhat senior position, and was therefore surrounded by even more and brighter lights than those in the outer office.

Sweeping aside the choir music lists which he was preparing for the coming Sunday, he made me most welcome, and the young lady immediately reappeared with a pot of tea for two, and half a Dundee cake. Curiously enough, our conversation didn't dwell on the super offices. We talked about church matters. His stories about the church council meetings at his parish church were very funny indeed. He said that they may have closed the local music-hall, but you could still see the best show ever at the PCC meetings, when the vicar wanted something done, and the other members didn't.

After a comfortable half-hour, George discovered that it was time to stop working for the day, and as I waited for him to have a wash and shave, I stood at the window and picked out the familiar sights of the town. There were the homely, crumbling rows of Victorian villas, the half demolished music-hall and the closed-down cinema. Below me, in the High Street, surged the usual fantastic traffic jam round the inevitable hole in the road. And further afield, beyond the all-but-defunct railway station and the completely defunct gasworks, I could see the town's three remaining trees. They stood defiantly in the peace of the asphalted churchyard. And there, of course, was the church itself. You couldn't miss it. It was a long thin building of violent yellow brick, and at one end it sprouted a quite unique erection that looked like a pepper-pot.

Returning to the office, and following the direction of my gaze, George explained urgently, 'I must get down there quickly. I've got a boys' choir practice in twenty minutes, and if I'm not there on time they'll probably smash every window in the place. Only last week they broke into the vestry and filled the piano with coke.' At my suggestion (for although George was proud of his office, he wasn't so sure about the choir vestry), I accompanied my friend to the practice. It was a pleasant relief from the generous glare of the Government electric light to pass into the hard-up glimmer of the church council's single 40-watt lamp.

We had arrived at the parish church in the nick of time. Most of the choirboys had organized themselves into a battering-ram team, and a disused flag pole from the pepper-pot tower was swinging impatiently between them, pointed directly at the vestry door. Only two or three boys dissociated themselves from this mob violence. They remained at a little distance, and appeared to be quietly and determinedly garrotting the solo boy. However, as soon as they realized that George was among them, they were all very considerate. The flag pole was put away tidily under the churchyard trees, and the solo boy and his would-be assassins romped into church in the most friendly way. George was delighted. He said that the feeling of a proud, happy community had even percolated down to these youngest townsfolk. Most of their fathers were now employed in some capacity in the new Government building, and their newborn joy and pride in their town was so great that it could not but affect their offspring. Time was, he assured me, when the boys would have carried on regardless with the battering while he stood there, and would have probably assassinated the solo boy as well (not that he would have blamed them after last Sunday's fiasco with 'O for the Wings of a Dove').

It was well past lighting-up time when we finished the practice. George expertly kicked the last boy out of the vestry and locked the door. As we walked down the road, he gazed up proudly at the glowing bulk of the Government building. I happened to glance back and, by its light, I imagined I saw a number of figures converging on a spot under the churchyard trees. At a little distance, two or three others appeared to be engaged in a life and death struggle.

16

Worship for His Worship

It was Mayor-Making Sunday at the parish church. This was the occasion when the new mayor and corporation made their annual appearance at choral Matins and the churchwardens and everybody in the choir had to turn up in force to create the illusion that they were always at all the other Matins when the mayor and corporation were not. Among the choir to whom, in the manner of choirs, nothing was sacred – not even mayors and corporations – the occasion was known as the visit of Ali Baba and the Forty Thieves.

As we waited in the vestry for the arrival of the honoured guests, the organist, an old friend of mine, said he was glad I'd decided to pay a visit on this particular Sunday because they were always sure of a jolly good show, for no matter how much the choir rehearsed all the moves and the music beforehand, there was always the certainty that someone would forget something and cause a right royal mess-up.

Everything possible was done for the enjoyment and comfort of the mayor and corporation. The same hymns were sung year after year so that they would feel at home and fully knowledgeable in church matters, and they were always provided with the hymn and prayer books which still boasted backs. They all sat in the four front pews right under the organ and the organist played so loudly that they were able to sing quite unselfconsciously without fear of hearing their own or the dreadful croak of the person next door.

The lessons were traditionally read by a large and very important alderman whose one ambition in life was to be heard. He therefore bawled every word in one shattering cannon-like boom as if he was announcing where the train standing at Platform 13 was going, and this so upset the young curate who rather fancied himself as a Shakespearean actor, that it took all his Christian courage to drag himself to the service and remain in a forgiving frame of mind till the end.

But the vicar loved the service. He loved the last-minute chaos in the vestry and the church filled with scarlet robes and uniforms and ridiculous hats. He loved to sit back entranced and hear the choir roar through Handel's 'Hallelujah' chorus, with the town brass band valiantly accompanying in a different key from the organ. As he always enthusiastically pointed out in his sermon, it was on such occasions that the church showed she was *alive* and *virile* and *united*. Without exception this kind of remark caused a bitter protest at the next church council meeting from the regular Matins congregation who imagined that the vicar was getting at them – just because they were nearly all over 70 and liked to sit as far as possible from each other and keep themselves to themselves. The vicar unfailingly explained that no offence was meant and asked, indeed, what would the Church of England do without such pillars of the church – such timeless stalwarts. And this, of course, made everything all right till the next mayor-making crisis.

At five minutes to eleven the choir formed up and processed into the chancel, there to await the arrival of the august procession from the town hall. The congregation stood as we entered and as nothing else seemed expected of them for a bit, all sat down again and continued shuffling their feet, dropping books and studying the ceiling. After what seemed an age of suspension when the organist had played 'The War March of the Priests' twice, and the 'Trumpet Voluntary' three times, the verger appeared at the back of the church to give the pre-arranged signal that the procession had arrived. Skilfully switching from the middle of Handel's 'Largo' to the opening line of 'Praise My Soul the King of Heaven' the organist led us into that great hymn, and there before us at last, in all their glory and fully 20 minutes late, appeared the mayor and corporation. They drifted dignified into their pews, a splendid heart-warming sight. Only one little alderman rather spoilt the picture. He wore a robe which seemed to have been made for a man eight feet tall, and he kept glaring behind him at the colleague who was trampling all over the yard or so which trailed along the floor. The little alderman didn't look very dignified, but the colleague did. He held his head high, took no notice and trampled on.

When everyone was seated, the mace-bearer, a vast gentleman wearing an expression of infinite sorrow

– obviously his special once-a-year church look – sadly fixed the mace into position along the mayor's pew. A choirboy in front of me gazed at it in wonder. 'Blimey!' he mused, 'Is that thing real gold?' The man next to me expertly dug him in the back with a psalter and the service continued merrily.

When we arrived at the spot when the notices are given out, the vicar glued his eyes to a half sheet of paper torn from an exercise book, and covered with atrocious black and red typing, with no full stops or commas. In one deep breath he announced that during the week the services would be as usual and there would be a jumble sale on Saturday afternoon in aid of the Graveyard Redevelopment Fund, and he would be pleased to receive any unwanted jumble at the vicarage during the week, and he was very glad to receive the mayor and corporation at church this morning.

In his sermon he said that despite little differences in the council chamber (these often went on into the small hours and ended up in vitriolic letters in the local paper), he knew that members of the borough council always strove to conduct the affairs of the borough in a true Christian spirit, each trying to understand the other's point of view, each putting the welfare of the borough before his or her personal feelings – all pulling together as a team . . .

Everyone put everything they had into the last hymn, 'Glorious Things of Thee are Spoken', and as usual, the town brass band completely drowned the organ. For years the band had tried to do the same thing with the other hymns and they had always come off second best.

But there was something about 'Glorious Things of Thee are Spoken'. Nothing could touch them on that one.

'Well, I thoroughly enjoyed it all,' I enthused to my friend the organist as we left the church '– and you can't say anyone made a right royal mess-up this year!'

'Oh! Can't I?' he retorted indignantly. He pointed to a tightly-closed circle of choirmen in the corner of the churchyard. 'I'll probably have a strike on my hands by tonight. They've all been victimized. Didn't you notice? The vicar went straight from the notices to the sermon. He didn't give us a chance to sing the "Hallelujah" chorus!'

17

Growler and Howler

The petrol station in the West Country village where my friend Harry, the village organist and choirmaster, is privileged to live is a sort of self-effacing, rustic affair known only to the locals. Far removed from the usual garish, arrogant eyesore that looks as though it's entirely made of multi-coloured plastic blocks and strips, there is nothing automatic or 'self-service' about this establishment. The proprietor, a large, ever-smiling middle-aged man deals personally with every customer and generally long discussions ensue covering everything from the Government's latest blunder to the mysterious failure of Granny Grundy's carrot crop.

Be it known that the proprietor also tracks down and brings back to life abandoned steam traction engines, rides a pet one-ton Shire horse for fun and is affectionately known as Growler owing to what Harry describes as his unique 'enraged football hooligan voice' which he exercises with awesome uninhibited fervour in the village church choir every Sunday. He is one of my all-time favourite characters except on the rather rare occasions when I am on a visit to Harry and join his choir for Sunday choral Matins. At such times

I unfailingly find myself placed next to Growler in the choir stalls where he unfailingly bellows and roars in my ears throughout the service with the result that I can't hear what the rest of the choir are doing and get rather lost not to say disorientated. But it is still good to witness Growler's dynamic enthusiasm. He appreciates being a member of Harry's choir above everything (except, perhaps, his ability to ride his Shire horse bareback across the Vicar's lawn at the parish fête) and his colleagues are ever ready to forgive him for wrecking their efforts Sunday after Sunday because he's such a happy-go-lucky, jolly fellow and keeps on inviting them round to his place for out-of-this world gourmet dinners lavishly provided by his equally jolly wife whose heaven on earth is her wondrous kitchen.

Ever cheerful as he appears, however, Growler is always much concerned over the health of his vocal chords, constantly on the alert for the slightest hint of a coming cold that could reduce the volume of his bear-like bass output. Each Sunday, therefore, the atmosphere in the choir stalls is permanently pervaded with the overpowering odour of Growler's latest cough lozenge or throat spray discoveries. This affects the rest of the choir not a jot (the vicar's warden has always said they're an utterly insensitive lot) but has been known to so upset some visiting preachers that their sermons have been reduced to incomprehensible splutterings followed by a hasty exit after the service in a desperate quest for fresh air.

One fine bright Sunday morning in January while on a rare visit to Harry I found myself in his choir vestry being fitted out with a spare cassock and surplice. The languid, quite beautiful soprano who Harry had called on to make me feel at home (a real friendly girl in a cool kind of way) held up a cassock in each hand. She said I was very welcome to either of them – one used to belong to a choirman who had grown so stout after he'd retired and sat watching television all day that he could no longer get into it and the other cassock had been left by a man who had heard a rumour that a lady priest was coming to the parish and went off to be a Roman Catholic. The soprano explained that this didn't matter very much because the man's voice had been almost as disruptive as Growler's and he didn't have a wife like Growler's to offer the choir the compensation of frequent gourmet dinners.

I chose the cassock of the man who was frightened of women priests and the languid, quite beautiful soprano further supplied me with a sparkling clean starched surplice and a delightful, all-embracing slow smile.

By now, more members of the choir had arrived, most of whom remembered me from previous visits and were most solicitous in their enquiries as to whether I had fully recovered from all the effects of my last visit when as usual someone had contrived to place me next to Growler for the singing of a particularly uninhibited festal choral evensong followed by encores of Handel's 'Hallelujah' chorus and 'Land of Hope and Glory'. Then, from the midst of that group of so kindly concerned gentlemen emerged a chorister I'd not seen before. She advanced on me with a military stride, a dramatic figure of generous girth and towering stature.

'Are you just a visitor or are you staying?' she demanded throatily.

I realized I'd automatically sprung to attention and my starched surplice crackled. 'I'm afraid I'm only . . .'

'What do you sing?' cut in the lady.

'Alto,' I responded smartly.

'I'm contralto,' she announced. 'You'll sit next to me.'

'With Growler on your other side!' purred the man next to me *sotto voce* as she moved away to order someone else about. 'She's only been here three months but she's made her voice heard,' continued my informant. I regarded him closely but he wasn't grinning. 'She suddenly came from nowhere, moved into the old station master's house and gave a lot of money to the organ fund. Then she joined the choir.'

'And she's a contralto?' I queried.

He thought for a while. 'I suppose it's a sort of female Growler noise,' he reckoned. 'We call her Howler.'

At the precise moment that the choir were about to process into the chancel to start the service Growler blundered into the vestry beaming hugely at everyone and tramping all over the fashionably shod feet of the languid, quite beautiful soprano who was far too languid to get out of his way. Following him to the robing cupboard serenely unaffected by the foot crushing, she proceeded leisurely and thoughtfully to array him in his cassock and surplice, surveying him critically and making adjustments until she was quite satisfied with his appearance. Meanwhile the vicar and choir waited and looked on patiently – except Howler the contralto who kept on sighing gustily and thumping the music cupboard door with a sturdy boot. 'Right! Grand! Off we go then!' coaxed the vicar eventually and we all trooped into the chancel and started the service with a great Victorian battle hymn 'Stand up! Stand up for Jesus'. We thundered with Growler and Howler battling it out well in the lead and the organ at full blast just about holding its own.

All went well until we reached the Te Deum which was to a setting by Stanford, a copy of which no one had given me. There came a great sigh next to me as I shuffled ineffectually among the various pieces of music on the desk before me. 'Share mine – hold it up,' hissed the contralto. I knew the setting quite well in fact but I didn't seem to recognize much of it as interpreted by the thunderous competition between Growler and Howler. I soon lost my place completely – only to be subjected to further humiliation as the lady glared at me and stabbed at the right place with a scarlet-nailed finger. And from then on I was under constant surveillance by Howler whose hand hovered over my music copies, ever ready to swoop on the next item to be sung and wave it under my chin. I acknowledged her help each time with a dutiful smile and she glared encouragingly. But her first concern was undoubtedly the pursuing of her 'who can bawl louder' contest with Growler on my other side and both acquitted themselves splendidly throughout the service. Transfixed between the giant and the giantess I was indeed witnessing a unique musical experience which far outshone the most way-out discords devised by some of our modern church composers.

By the end of the service my ears buzzed as they do when I pass a battery of pneumatic drills digging an emergency hole in the road for the gas company. Only as the buzzing subsided did I realize that Growler was inviting me to join the rest of the choir for one of his wife's famous gourmet dinners after evensong. 'I won't take no for an answer,' he was booming, 'everybody will be there and that includes you.'

At the dinner (and what a dinner!) Growler's wife put me next to the languid, quite beautiful soprano, for which I was most grateful. On my other side sat a small, elderly choirman who had placed a pocketful of coins on the table and was engrossed in sorting them into two piles. He said he'd just returned from a holiday in Italy and had got his remaining foreign coins mixed up with his English money and had that morning been almost accused of trying to pass dud cons at the newsagents.

I saw that my friend Harry, the organist, was seated at the top of the table between Growler and Howler. My relief must have shown on my face. 'Better him than you?' whispered the languid, quite beautiful soprano. And from then on, although from time to time some loud noises and even scraps of strange disharmony reached us near the bottom of the table, we managed a peaceful most enjoyable meal. The man with the left-over foreign coins got them all sorted out between courses and the soprano, learning that I was a cat lover, became much less languid explaining that she also was mad about cats, and had three gorgeous, hefty black and white tom moggies who ruled her life – 'my babies', she called them.

'You must meet them when this is over,' she invited. And so it was. There in the front room of her delightful cottage the monstrous 'babies' sat about fatly. In the discerning manner of cats they recognized another cat lover and gave me the most wonderful tail-in-the-air, head-butting purring welcome. During his ecstatic movements one of them knocked over a pile of CDs. As I bent to retrieve them one featuring a famous Austrian brass band caught my eye. 'One of my great favourites,' said the soprano over my shoulder. 'Unusual, I suppose, but I love brass bands – especially Austrian ones.'

'Put it on,' I said.

'More loud noise after all you've been through to-night?' she queried, and her smile was magic.

'You should know,' I told her, 'that every summer I go to a small village in the Austrian Salzkammergut just to sit in the village square each evening and listen to the band.'

A moment later the whole place thundered with Johann Strauss's 'Radetzky March'. It was much, much louder than the combined efforts of Growler and Howler – but then I *love* Austrian brass bands.

18

The Choir Will Now Sing

The annual Choir Benefit Evensong was the terrible occasion when every single member of the village choir turned up, and the congregation were subjected to the most uninhibited rendering of Handel's 'Let their celestial concerts all unite' and, for some extraordinary reason, a really jolly interpretation of 'Art thou weary, art thou languid'. This was supposed to make them so grateful to the choir that they simply poured money into the collection at the close of the service and thus enabled the choir to embark once again on their glorious, traditional seaside outing and dinner.

For over half a century the choir had enjoyed this event. For over half a century the villagers had been awakened at an unearthly hour on the first Saturday in June by the sounds of the choir preparing to leave on their journey. The sounds consisted of the clatter of beer crates being loaded into the back of a conveyance, and the hoarse voice of the organist bellowing bloodcurdling and quite unrealistic threats at the junior members of the choir who were chasing each other backwards and forwards across the police sergeant's front garden flower beds and up and down Queen Victoria's Golden Jubilee commemoration oak tree.

The Benefit Evensong had been instituted by a large, sporting Edwardian vicar, who adored brass bands, couldn't read a note of music and thought the choir was marvellous, and the tradition was reluctantly continued by a small, modern vicar whose idea of heaven was to listen to hours of plainsong, had written a book on Tudor madrigals, and thought the choir was quite shocking.

For years he had tried discreetly to discourage parishioners from joining the choir by offering the likely ones time-filling jobs as servers and Sunday School teachers. But he had been markedly unsuccessful. They didn't want to serve or teach. They just wanted to bawl in the choir. And meanwhile existing members of the choir kept on marrying each other and raising families, all of whom were automatically squeezed into the choir stalls as soon as they could read.

So the small modern vicar suffered on, and dutifully announced year after year on Low Sunday that 'as a mark of our great appreciation for all the sterling, faithful work the choir continues to put in, I am indeed happy to remind you that there will be the usual Choir Benefit Evensong next Sunday, and I am sure that all of us will want to support it with our presence and our money'.

It was said by some of the more uncharitable members of the choir that the vicar tried his hardest to get himself invited out as a visiting preacher at some neighbouring church on the fateful Sunday, but he was finding it harder and harder to do this, owing to the fact that the neighbouring churches had all experienced solid half-hour examples of his visiting preaching. Besides, it was always the same sermon: 'When your vicar so kindly invited me to preach here tonight, I felt honoured – honoured and happy. As I stand in this ancient parish church, I sense all around me that wonderful surge of Christian friendship and unity . . .'

On the particular Sunday when I had been invited by my friend the organist to take part in the Benefit Evensong the weather was really beautiful and the day had, in fact, been hotter than normal for early June. The sun was still blistering the tarmac in the village street. The first thing that I noticed, apart from the noise and utter chaos, when I entered the vestry was the stifling, jungle-like heat. This, I soon learned from an ancient tenor gentleman, was mainly attributable to a possibly even more ancient black iron electric fire, a fearsome contraption, which took up one entire corner of the vestry and appeared to be switched full on. Apparently it was always switched full on.

'You see,' explained the ancient one, 'the socket is connected to the electric light circuit, so every time we turn on the lights the fire comes on as well.'

He perhaps noticed a certain puzzlement on my face. He spoke carefully, slowly, rather in the manner of a teacher explaining a simple, obvious point to a particularly dim-witted child. 'The plug's stuck, you see – has been for years – and the socket has seen its best days, so we can't really force the plug out.' He gazed admiringly at the sagging, dull red elements and the vast expanse of rusty iron. 'They don't make fires like that nowadays,' he said nostalgically. 'It's nice to see it glowing. We don't get much warm weather nowadays, anyway. Now when I was a boy . . .'

But I never heard what it was like when he was a boy. We were swept apart as the organist suddenly materialized in the midst of the mass of singers sweltering round the fire, and started handing out copies of 'Let the celestial concerts all unite'. My copy was typical of the copies of well-loved church anthems. Use by generations of choristers had reduced it to a limp, rag-like texture, and all over the front cover the titles of hundreds of the publisher's other anthems were advertised. The only trouble was that the print was so minute that you needed either exceptional eyesight or a microscope to read it.

And in my copy someone had added some highly original musical directions to the score. Warnings such as 'Watch it!' and 'Come in *loud* here' and 'Don't hang on' and 'Don't listen to the basses' were all over the place. There were also a number of firm orders saying '*Don't* take a breath'. These extended over four pages of music and, as far as I could make out, if you did what you were told you'd end up suffocated. Anyway, it wasn't for me to question the wisdom of the ages, and I was quite willing to try my luck at not breathing for a bit and not listening to the basses if it helped in the effort to extract cash from the congregation for such a worthy cause as the annual outing.

My friend the organist who revered tradition and, throughout a succession of musically advanced vicars, had always devoutly hoped that the next one would be less of a nuisance to the choir than the present one, was giving his final instructions about the singing of the anthem – the same final instructions that he'd given for decades. 'So,' he concluded, wiping perspiration from his forehead with a large, faded red handkerchief, 'let it really go, but *do* hold back some of the beef for the last page. We don't want everything to start fizzling out on the last page. We want to finish with a *bang*.'

The vicar, whose desperate efforts to get invited absolutely anywhere as a visiting preacher had failed and whose heavy cold of yesterday, which could have kept him in bed, had miraculously vanished overnight, stood quietly and bravely before us. 'I am sure', he said, with that earnestness which he tried to put into everything, 'that the music tonight will be a great success and enjoyed by all, particularly if we all remember to – er – moderate slightly our – er – natural exuberance in such hymns as "Art thou weary".'

His voice was drowned in the first pulverizing chords of the piece the organist always played at the Benefit Evensong. As we processed into church the change in temperature from the tropical vestry to the dim coolness of the chancel was quite breathtaking. I found myself sitting next to the ancient tenor, 'You should be here in winter,' he said, as we turned to the first hymn. 'Talk about cold! I don't know what we'd do without that old fire. They don't make 'em like that nowadays . . .'

19

The End of the Line

One day when I was young . . .

Rather surprisingly even for those days the Somerset village where I spent a short holiday was still mercifully in the Dark Ages, boasting no new bungalow estates, new trunk roads, skyscrapers or nuclear power stations. Following my usual custom I had got myself invited into the local church choir but was disappointed to learn that owing to the clergy shortage the church was only open Sunday morning, while Evensong was sung in the church of a neighbouring village. However, the same choir and organist served both places, and a choirgirl who, like myself, turned out to be a railway enthusiast, suggested that we should make the evening journey by the local train on the preserved steam line run by enthusiasts which was much more interesting than the local bus, and far safer than the organist's car.

The station, which was situated in the middle of a field, was known endearingly as Grinding Halt. It was a most picturesque establishment with a booking-office containing no booking-clerk, and a waiting-room containing no seats. On the platform a large Boxer dog stood studying the timetable. Perhaps he understood it because he looked very intelligent, but to my un-mathematical mind the hundreds of figures, lines, dots and pointing hands suggested nothing but a printer's nightmare.

The choirgirl understood it however, and said that it simply meant that there were three trains a day which ran whenever the engine driver felt in the mood. While we waited she further explained that we didn't need tickets, as everybody paid at the other end, and that we were certain of getting there in time for the service because her brother, who was the fireman, was also the only bass in the choir, and managed to work in Even-song with his stoking.

True enough, the train soon appeared, the stout snuffling little engine looking remarkably like the Boxer dog who now abandoned the timetable and lumbered down the platform and on to the track, regarding the train with a worried frown. The two carriages were packed solid with three regular passengers, the engine driver's bike, and about 150 steam railway enthusiasts from London who had heard a rumour that the line was to close and wanted to make sure of 'doing the run'. It took a little time for the guard to ease us into the last compartment, where I had to stand with bowed head to avoid hitting the richly decorated ceiling which must have been the pride of the 1870s. Then the Boxer dog stood aside and we were on our way.

The choirgirl's brother coped splendidly with the stoking, for in no time at all we shuddered to a halt at the end of the line, which appeared to be the church graveyard. The three regular passengers who were also choir members joined us, and having paid our fares to a porter who held out his hand and never looked at what we gave him, we all climbed over a wall and dodged through the tombs to the vestry.

In the vestry we came upon the organist imparting last-minute instructions about the anthem to a dangerous looking mob of choirboys who were taking no notice whatsoever. He was an imposing figure wearing a deep frown and red carpet clippers. The choirgirl had explained that he always wore the frown owing to his contact with generations of moronic trebles. He always wore the carpet slippers also, but no one quite knew why. He seemed pleased to see me again and was, I think, about to try his last-minute anthem briefing on me, but had to excuse himself hurriedly to reprimand one of the boys who was wearing somebody else's surplice back to front.

Meanwhile, a choirman handed me a yellowing sheet of paper advertising a jumble sale of ten years ago on the back of which was a spidery collection of numbers and letters. He announced briefly, 'That's what we're singing' and cuffing a boy out of his way, passed on. My choirgirl friend, who could see that I hadn't the faintest idea of how to translate the jumble into music, once again came to my rescue. She revealed that this was the hymn list, and as it was almost unknown for the choir to use the tune set to a hymn, the hymn number was put first, followed by the initials of the hymnal. These were followed by the location of the tune. Sometimes the tune or hymn was in the manuscript form and this, of course, further complicated the list. I suggested that this was all rather unusual, but she explained it away with a charming simplicity.

She said the vicar was one of those who like to show how broadminded they are by working regardlessly through almost every hymn in the book – and some outside as well. And the choir was one of those who only know about a dozen tunes which have been handed down from generation to generation, and strongly object to learning anything else. Consequently a most keen and enjoyable contest had developed between the vicar and the organist. The vicar would dig up an unknown hymn, and the organist would endeavour to fit it to one of the choir's accepted tunes. The organist and choir had never been beaten, but once they had been in grave danger of losing a point. The vicar had discovered a hymn written in such an extraordinary metre that it refused to be married off to an eligible tune.

Things looked black, and it became obvious that the choir would have to do the unthinkable and learn a new tune. However, at the last moment, the vicar was taken ill with 'flu, and a relieving priest had been prevailed upon to substitute 'Onward, Christian Soldiers'.

I remember little of the actual service except that I found a firm friend in the fireman who had got rid of his engine and sat next to me in the stalls. During the sermon we discovered that we were both fiercely *Ancient & Modern (Standard Edition)* men.

My day was made!

20

The Bulldozing Bass

In the wilds of Norfolk there is a village where they are
so far behind the times that the vicar has never been able
to persuade a single parishioner to be cremated. And the
churchyard is now so overcrowded they've had to take
over the adjoining site of the proposed rural crafts centre as an extension. The site of the proposed rural crafts
centre had been there, awaiting developments on the
parish council, and covered with four-foot-high weeds
and old mattresses, for 25 years, and most people had
long forgotten that it was the proposed site of anything,
so the change in its proposed use didn't upset anyone.

The principal bass in the village church choir was, in
fact, overjoyed about the idea. He ran a small electrical shop in the High Street and, in most ways, was a
perfectly normal man, with a perfectly normal village
church bass voice which drowned every other voice in
the choir and shattered the vicar's wife's nervous system
every time they sang 'Now thank we all Our God'.

But he had one peculiarity. He had a mania for attending auctions and acquiring large cumbersome articles
for which he had no use whatsoever.

His wife, who adored him and considered him the

greatest bass since Chaliapin, had for years picked her way through an almost impenetrable maze of old tricycles, gigantic worn out water tanks, rusty baths and pensioned-off lamp posts, to hang out her washing at the bottom of the garden. And never once in their 30 years of married life had she complained. She thought that all great artists differed in their habits from ordinary mortals, and she was rather proud of her husband's habits.

Then, one day, he went to a builder's auction and brought home a sort of baby bulldozer, which knocked down the front gate posts on its way in, shattered the coal shed and tore up half the garden path. The principal bass was extremely proud of the baby bulldozer. He stood enraptured, gazing at it as it crouched in the midst of a mangled pile of wreckage in the back garden. He lifted the remains of two formerly well-loved Edwardian tricycles and the coal shed door from its bulk. This was his finest hour. This was the ultimate. What could compare, even faintly, with the baby bulldozer? Not the tricycles. Not the pensioned-off lamp posts or even the rusty baths, fascinating as they were. Not the worn out water tanks – not even *gigantic* worn out water tanks. The baby bulldozer was supreme.

But you can't just stand and watch such an appealing thing. You get an overpowering urge to use it – to sit aloft and drive triumphantly through brick walls and level-crossing gates and bus shelters where you've waited for hours for mysterious buses which have never turned up.

The principal bass realized that he could never do

123

any of these things, yet for him a great and compensating opportunity was just around the corner. He never listened to the notices for the week which the vicar read out in church each Sunday, because he wasn't interested in Young Wives' meetings, coffee mornings or parish visits to stately homes and plastics factories, but on one particular morning the vicar was talking about the extension of the churchyard and he caught the words 'clear up the country crafts site'.

It was enough. It was a golden godsend. Five minutes after Morning Service had ended he had bulldozed the vicar into letting him clear every single weed and mattress from the site.

Quite unaware of these thrilling developments, I was in the vicinity of the village one autumn afternoon and decided to call on the principal bass in his electrical shop. He had always been most helpful to me whenever I had been a guest in the choir. During Service he had never failed to pass along a tin of throat sweets every two minutes, and had always insisted in the most unselfish way that I should have the hymn book with the cover. The throat sweets were so violent that they brought tears to my eyes and nearly choked me, and the hymn book had half its pages missing, but I did appreciate his kind thoughts and we became very friendly. When I arrived at his shop, he was dealing with a large fur-coated lady with mauve hair who was just telling him he was the biggest fool in Christendom, or something to that effect, because he had apparently said that he couldn't repair her venerable electric kettle which had no handle, was full of fur, and had a hole in the bottom.

The principal bass transferred his beam to me. 'Oh she's all right really,' he assured me. 'She'll be back. She always gets a bit annoyed about prices, but she's quite a good customer really. She buys no end of unrepeatable bargains at the Annual Slightly Soiled Sale. Last year she simply *grabbed* a washing machine that had fallen off a lorry. She sends all her laundry out, but she just couldn't resist the rock-bottom, giveaway-price. Of course she kicks up about one or two bargains when she gets them home, but as long as I take them back she always buys a load more at the next Slightly Soiled Sale. Quite a good customer really!' When I told him I had a few hours to spare he became quite flatteringly overjoyed. 'I've got something to *show* you,' he said tensely, and between customers and telephone calls I heard the saga of the baby bulldozer, and accepted an invitation to tea and afterwards to 'help' him in the clearing of the country crafts site. He said he wanted to show me how easy it would all be with the baby bulldozer. He said I was very lucky to have happened along at that particular time. Another day and the job would have been done and I would have missed a terrific thrill . . .

After tea we prepared for the terrific thrill. From his garden shed the principal bass unearthed a voluminous, damp-smelling boiler suit full of patches and tears and eminently suited to someone seven feet tall with a girth like a gas holder. He draped me in this and adjusted it at the back with some delicately tinted pink ribbon which he ripped from a birthday card depicting horses and roses and great red hearts which, for some reason, was pinned up in the shed. 'Splendid!' he pronounced.

'And you'd better slip these on. There's rather a lot of stinging nettles and broken glass and things on the site and *your* shoes won't be much protection.' And he handed me what appeared to be a pair of ancient rubber boots with the tops torn off. I'd never seen him so happy. 'Now let's go,' he beamed. 'The bulldozer's in the graveyard.'

If you are not used to walking in ancient waders full of stones, dried mud and bits of rolled up cardboard, you perhaps find it a little difficult to progress very speedily, but such was the enthusiasm of the principal bass that I found myself almost running with him to the churchyard. Anyway, we arrived at a smart trot. 'There!' He pointed proudly at the monstrous baby bulldozer, wedged against a large flamboyant vault. He picked up a sizeable piece of marble and tossed it into some long grass. 'A corner of the vault came off as I drove past,' he explained. 'Fancy putting the thing so near the path as that.'

He invited me to 'jump' on the back of the bulldozer, and in a splendidly satanic cloud of black diesel fumes, we careered through the graveyard to an opening in the wall which gave on to the country crafts site.

I was glad of the waders. They certainly protected much of me from the nettles. It was really no one's fault that the baby bulldozer suddenly lurched into an unseen hole and enabled the nettles to smartly whip our faces, but, as the principal bass so cheerily pointed out, that was all part of the fun of it.

The baby bulldozer was an energetic and tireless worker. It heaved tons of rubbish and roots from one side of the site to the other and back again. It hurled down an entire wall and sent a ton weight Shire horse in the next field cantering in a frenzy all over the vicar's prize carnations. And it enlarged the original hole into something ten times its size, finally trapping itself at the bottom with eight mattresses, a car with no wheels and about a dozen and a half saucepans which had seen their best days.

'This is what I've always enjoyed,' roared the principal bass above the paralyzing pounding of the engine. 'Working in the open air!'

The diesel fumes curled around us and billowed upwards, almost enveloping a figure who had suddenly appeared at the edge of the crater. It wore a large fur coat and had mauve hair. It wildly waved a battered electric kettle.

The principal bass shut off the engine.

'*There* you are,' the lady was screaming. 'The vicar said I'd find you here. *What* are you supposed to be doing now? For goodness sake!'

The principal bass turned up to her his beaming countenance and rose from the driving seat. 'And what can I do for you, madam?' he enquired.

'I've decided to buy a new kettle,' she announced imperiously. 'You're a robber but there it is. That is what we have to put up with these days. I want it *now*. How much will you allow me on the old one?'

Nothing and no one could ruffle the principal bass. The baby bulldozer had filled his life with unassailable happiness. 'I'll come back to the shop with you immediately!' he soothed. He scrambled to the top of the crater where the lady stood back and inspected his filth-covered form with disgust.

'I shan't be long,' he called back to me. He gazed longingly at the baby bulldozer. 'Let her cool off for a bit. Don't touch her controls.'

I had a curious reluctance to touch anything on this terrible delight of his heart. Gently I pulled at one of the mattresses – a double-bed one – in an effort to clear a way out of the crater which my waders could negotiate. It moved quite easily and released an avalanche of rubble over me. I picked myself up and was vaguely pleased to see another and larger avalanche descend on the baby bulldozer.

I wasn't there when the principal bass returned.

He wrote to me later and wasn't the slightest annoyed with me. It seemed that the baby bulldozer had given not only lasting happiness but tremendous enthusiasm to his whole life – enthusiasm which was abundantly evident in everything he did. Apparently he had just sung the bass solo in Goss's 'Wilderness' with such vigour that even the deaf church warden who always sat in the very back pew and complained that he couldn't hear a thing, said he heard the solo *quite* distinctly, and the vicar reckoned *he'd* never heard anything like it in his whole life.

21

Compromise

Over the phone, Rupert, another of my village church choir reporters, told me, 'At choir practice last night our organist took us through the musical programme that's wanted for our next choral wedding. The bride wants to come down the aisle with "When the Saints go Marching in" and the bridegroom wants the next hymn to be "Fight the Good Fight" followed by "Oft in Danger, Oft in Woe". Then during the signing of the register the bride's father wants us to sing "The Battle Hymn of the Republic" – you know, "John Brown's Body". And at the end they'll all process out of the church with Mendelssohn's "War March of the Priests".'

'This is all a somewhat unusual choice of music for a wedding,' I ventured.

'Well, the happy couple are very enthusiastic, indeed very insistent about it,' he said. 'They like the *tunes*, y'see. It's the *tunes* that count. They're both from military families from way back. There's memorial plaques all over the church walls to a great grandfather, two grandfathers and there are four other relatives who did their stuff in the Crimean War or got mixed up in the Boer War.' Rupert recalled the reason why he was phoning me, 'Anyway, apart from all that, this wedding takes place on Saturday week and it's going to be a big showy affair with a big showy congregation and so they want a big choir.'

'A big *showy* choir,' I presumed.

'Exactly,' he agreed, 'and we can put up a good show – with our sopranos at least. We've only got two boys but we've got a dozen or so ladies including some who can sing and they all look very attractive in the front choir stalls. Our contraltos are all right too when they're not looking aggressive because they don't like a male alto (me) invading their pitch – although there is one contralto who doesn't seem to mind my voice at all but most of the time she sings soprano without knowing it.' Rupert sighed gustily, 'But the men are the trouble because most of them won't be there. Three tenors are on holiday and that's all of them and we have two basses but one is taking his pet Shire horse to a big horse show that he never misses where he always wins the challenge cup, well, the horse does. The other bass will be around but he can't read music and only sings out when there's another bass bawling next to him to give him confidence. There are one or two other men but we only see them when the local football or cricket team are not playing at home. So – I wondered if you'd like to come down here and help me out. I've got one or two other pals lined up!' His enthusiastic voice was encouraging. 'I know that you don't drive but we've got a train down here that has somehow evaded the rail "modernizers" so it still actually runs – on time too!'

Of course, I went.

I arrived at Rupert's village station just one hour before the big service. The clanking, cheerful-looking little train got there dead on time and the handful of passengers were greeted by an actual visible porter instead of a safety camera and a recorded warning to mind the gap between the train and the platform. He paused in his task of painting a door marked 'Lamps', beamed on us, an ancient crumpled cherub, and said it was 'all going on' just up the road there at the church. For me it was like being back in the old days – so very comfortable and pleasant.

I made my way directly to the choir vestry and, although I'd never visited this particular vestry before, I felt immediately at home.

From one entire wall a large gathering of historic vicars and organists frowned or glared down on me from dark paintings and huge sepia photographs interspersed with notices about forthcoming local flower, horse and dog shows, reminders to the choir to make sure their surplices were presentably washed and ironed for Easter Sunday, a list of the choir darts team and an appeal to those choir members who read their Sunday papers during the sermon to please do so more discreetly because, even with the choir screen conveniently in the way it was still possible for members of the congregation to notice wads of paper being waved around.

The choir robes cupboard spanned the wall below the portraits (they must have had a huge choir here years ago) but now half the space was taken up with a smart bicycle and two skateboards and one of the huge photos of historic vicars that a broken picture cord had apparently deposited into the robes cupboard. The fallen vicar leaned unsteadily against the bicycle, and glared at people's feet. A battered table stood in one corner next to an even more battered piano. Brilliant beams of sunlight through the rose tinted glass of mullioned windows revealed golden dust hovering over them both.

Now the place was filled with regular choir members trying to fit out the special wedding choir visitors with cassocks and surplices that vaguely fitted them and were not too obviously pensioned-off garments from another generation. Beside the veteran piano the organist, an immaculate figure of authority recognizable by his silk musician's gown was loudly commanding a choirboy who was sucking at the soggy remains of an ice cream and chocolate cornet to 'throw the disgusting mess into the waste bin, go and wash your filthy paws and revolting visage and introduce a comb to your horrible hair – and congratulations, again, boy, on your solo "Ave Maria" last Sunday. Almost perfect. Splendid!'

Rupert materialized, easing his way between the piano and a huge man who was endeavouring to retie his shoelace from a standing position, there being no seats handy. 'Oh, you made it. Fine!' he greeted me. 'It's not so crowded in here generally but of course today we've got to get all these extras looking as if they are singers. The vicar found most of them. Heaven knows from where or whether any of 'em can sing.' The man tying his shoelace overbalanced and we helped him up. Rupert went on, 'I asked one of 'em if she sang soprano or contralto and she said, "yes".'

A minute or two later the vicar, a sprightly bird-like lady of uncertain age and immediate vigorous charm, wearing a rusty black cassock and large shapeless sandals, edged her way into the choir vestry and chirruped excitedly. 'She's here! The bride has arrived early! She's now being waylaid outside by the photographers. We'd better get into place quickly.' The silk-clad organist was already at the keyboard producing tremendous heroic Wagnerian rumblings with something from *The Twilight of the Gods* so we sorted ourselves out – with Rupert as far as possible away (behind a pillar actually) from the contralto ladies his voice so upset and the rest of the men fronted by our glamorous soprano line-up whose appearance, as the man next to me observed, 'really did the choir proud'. Good looks like theirs often cover a multitude of musical sins in church choirs.

The chancel that housed the choir was considerably raised from the nave where the wedding party had gathered and was partially cut off by a substantial oak choir screen which for the occasion had been literally curtained with exotic flowers so that from our deep high-backed choir stalls we had but a limited view of proceedings. We caught sight of gorgeous uniforms and a sea of sunshade-sized ladies' hats. A magnificent Alsatian wearing a brass studded collar and silk scarf bearing some regimental colours elegantly negotiated the flowered screen and inspected the choir closely before returning to the congregation apparently satisfied that it was in order for us to be there on this very upmarket occasion.

With military precision the ceremony got under

way right on time. The bride, having been reluctantly released by the photographers, was on her father's arm ready with the saints to go marching in, although when she moved forward she appeared to float, rather than march, a move that didn't exactly enhance the overall military effect. Through the curtain of flowers on the choir screen I had a clear if much restricted view of the vicar as she faced the bride and groom and was surprised to note that in the traditional fashion show atmosphere, she hadn't changed her rusty cassock and her surplice, although shining white, appeared to have been borrowed from an exceptionally diminutive choirboy. Following the direction of my prying gaze, the choirman next to me nudged me. 'She always wears that cassock,' he explained, 'does her gardening, shopping, car repairs, fishing, carting her rubbish to the tip – all in that cassock. It's as if she's inspired by it. She's not one of your modern types who only slip on a plastic clerical collar when they conduct a service and the rest of the time go about disguised as a raver at a Pop Festival.'

The service moved along smartly with cameras flashing from all over the church while vows were made, various members of the colourful congregation declaimed or stumbled through passages from celebrated literary works including some from what seemed to be the most blood curdling parts of the Old Testament. Then, during the signing of the register the choir came into their own again with a vigorous rendering of 'The Battle Hymn of the Republic' and a roving photographer attracted by the resultant uproar behind the choir screen had crept through it on his hands and knees to investigate only to be gently but firmly eased out of the way by the magnificent Alsatian with the regimental scarf. As the photographer backed off through the flower curtain his place was taken by an exquisite looking child of about four years – a little girl in a crisp Tyrolean dress. She placed an arm affectionately around the Alsatian's massive shoulders and they stood together, these two, quite still, regarding the choir with bright-eyed concentration. I found myself holding up my hymn book and singing with a new enthusiasm and the contralto who mostly sang soprano suddenly started to sing contralto.

Later, after the organist had excelled himself by playing 'The War March of the Priests' three times over in order to get everybody out of the church and into the big marquee next door in a harmonious frame of mind, I joined Rupert and regular choir members in the comparatively peaceful atmosphere of the choir vestry where the vicar joined us. 'Wonderful! Wonderful!' she enthused. 'You know, at the end of every service where you all sing so *inspiringly* I am always left just that *little* bit sad that once again the congregation have been denied the privilege of *fully* enjoying our superb efforts, because of that awful intrusive choir screen.'

'Here we go again,' whispered Rupert to me. 'This kind of thing is liable to go on and on. A very nice woman, mind you, but when she gets an idea into her head – oh dear!'

'You see, as we are seated at the family service these days,' pursued the vicar earnestly, 'choir and congregation are almost two separate entities divided under one roof. You all must have noticed the little girl at the wedding who actually "found" the choir. Children are full of curiosity. She *discovered* the choir when she went on an investigative tour of the church! There should have been no need at all. Choir and congregation should have been singing *together* united in praise.' The vicar smiled encouragingly, doubtless hoping for even a slender sign of support for her view although she knew quite well that the choir were loath to give up their comfortable secluded stalls to come down and perch on the yellow plastic chairs with nowhere to put your hymn book that she had recently introduced for the congregation in place of a number of removed pews.

There was what is often referred to as an uneasy silence and in an effort to move things along I said, 'If I as a visitor may say a word, I was most impressed by the actions of the splendid Alsatian.'

'Ah, yes, indeed, Karl our parish warden's dog,' agreed the vicar promptly. 'Karl is wonderful – so understanding. He is really the *only* link between the choir and the congregation during a service. He patrols, very unobtrusively between the two entities. In his mind we are all one family you see. Would that we all could realize and appreciate this truth and act on it as does Karl.' She paused and smiled at us again despite detecting no immediate reaction (she was, after all, used to detecting no immediate reaction before the choir eventually disagreed with whatever she had suggested) and went on with rising excitement, 'and of course, with the choir and congregation sitting together, no longer divided by the deadening screen, our wonderful organist would be in charge of the singing of *everyone*, not just the choir. And under the tuition of such a charismatic music director we would (among other things) soon become a first-rate choral society – well, if not *immediately* a first-rate society, certainly a second-rate one – no! that doesn't sound quite right, does it, but you know what I mean.'

The man who had stood next to me at the wedding service whispered, 'What will she think of next? She's not safe to be around unsupervised.'

Unexpectedly, the contralto who mostly sang soprano said slowly, 'Well, I suppose our organist *could* work a kind of magic with the congregation. I've never thought of him as charismatic though. If we didn't get on with him as well as we do I suppose we'd regard him as a martinet.'

'Or just a straightforward, self-opinionated bully,' put in one of the glamorous front-row sopranos who was adjusting her latest fake eye-lashes before the vestry's spotty mirror.

'You're dead right there,' agreed Rupert, regarding her admiringly.

'But absolutely fascinating,' continued the soprano. 'He makes choir practice *really* entertaining. You never know who he's going to pick on next or how outrageous he'll be. He makes each practice an exciting experience – gets away with murder. I like him.'

'And so do the rest of us – secretly,' mused Rupert, 'we're lucky to have him.'

The glamorous soprano finally appeared satisfied with her latest eye-lashes. She turned from the spotty mirror with a sudden startled movement. 'But can you imagine the situation if the vicar gets her way and this organist we all love so dearly actually starts telling the congregation what he thinks of their singing in his own endearing, straightforward way? What about that lady who sits at the back of the church – Lady Battleaxe – who reports to the vicar everyone who arrives late for the service – what about her being told her singing voice is like unto that of an ageing corncrake? And what if the vicar's warden, the Major, is ordered to stand up straight and hold his book up . . .?'

The vicar had a good sense of humour and imagination. She laughed unreservedly at the situations conjured up by the glamorous soprano. 'Look, I can't hang around here all day listening to you facetious lot,' she announced. 'I must put in an appearance at the wedding party next door.'

After she'd gone the facetious lot continued to hang around in the choir vestry becoming more and more facetious and were still there when the vicar returned. 'It's so good to see how much you all love this place,' she twinkled, 'and as you are still here I wonder if you'd like to hear my alternative plan for togetherness of choir and congregation.' No one actually said no so the vicar took the floor. 'This was suggested to me by one of the wedding guests who, by the way, liked the idea of the choir invisible. He thought it dramatic. Being realistic, I realize I suppose, that my idea of the choir leaving their stalls and coming down among the congregation will take a generation or two to become reality. Meanwhile, all is not lost. What do you say to this procedure? At Sunday evensong the congregation

138

is much smaller than at the morning service and the space between the choir stalls is quite large enough to accommodate three or four short rows of chairs so that the whole congregation could come up and join the choir – all praising together, you see.'

Her voice took on a sudden note of no-nonsense finality. 'You lot *must* surely see that here we have a solution.' She smiled a sort of triumphant little smile and was gone. We soon followed her, still in a group, out into the churchyard.

'That's really not a bad idea,' considered Rupert. 'A little compromise on our part like having people up in the choir perched on yellow plastic chairs with nowhere to put their hymn books may sound daft but it'll work wonders with the vicar. She's a nice person and she won't want to upset the choir with any more forward thinking notions – for a while at least. And it'll be alright about us reading Sunday papers during the sermon as we only do that at the morning service, don't we.'

A highly respected, white-haired contralto lady who had hitherto not joined the facetious discussion (she was never facetious but she gave the most gorgeous choir dinners twice a year at the manor house) now spoke firmly, authoritatively. 'We are fortunate indeed in these difficult times to have such an excellent vicar – a woman. In my experience woman priests are on the whole splendidly successful because they have such a capacity for sympathetic understanding of parish matters, a wonderful reassuring attitude to traditionalists who fear change. They have so much insight, so much loving understanding . . .'

'So much push,' concluded the glamorous soprano, elbowing a couple of scuffling choirboys out of her path.

22

A Trying Day

One snowbound morning in the middle of the coldest winter for half a century, I was cheered by a letter from an old friend I had known when he first became a curate, and who had recently attained his first vicarage. It was on a new estate outside a well known Bedfordshire town.

'Do come along, and see me,' he had written. 'Do come! This estate is so ghastly that you'd never credit it unless you actually saw it.' Naturally I could not resist such an attractive invitation, so a few days later, on a Wednesday afternoon, I was being put off a bus into a foot or so of slush and ice, which the town council apparently lacked the money, labour and inclination to clear. I felt immediately the warm welcome of the new estate.

My friend had explained that it really consisted of two sections, one built by private enterprise and the other by the council. They blended very well, the only difference between them being that, whereas the private planners had wavered between three distinct types of domestic monstrosity, the council had firmly made up their minds and settled for one. The resulting nightmare was a vast acreage of yellow bricks and wire fencing, intersected by charming concrete roads. And these were tastefully lined by concrete lamp standards, cunningly fashioned on eighteenth-century gibbets.

The whole scene was very peaceful. Indeed, the only living being in sight was a milkman who appeared to be making some unprintable remarks to himself about his electric milk float, which was stuck firmly in the fallen remains of a magnificent snowman.

As a friendly prelude to enquiring the way to St Margaret's Church, I leant my shoulder quite unavailingly to the back of the milk float, and told the milkman he'd never have had this trouble if the dairy company had stuck to horses. But I don't think it was quite the right thing to say just then, because his unprintable remarks became even more unprintable, and he didn't seem the least interested in horses. However, he did seem to know where the church was. He kindly directed me to a spot a half a mile away on the very top of a hill where the estate petered out in the corporation rubbish dump. I don't mind a good stiff walk and I certainly got one now. Within a few minutes, feeling very much warmer, I was standing in a snowdrift before the church. It was new and clean, and suitably hideous, and it wasn't St Margaret's at all.

It was St Michael's. It was firmly bolted and barred, and its main door bore a heart-warming message which said something about everybody being very welcome.

I couldn't find another milkman or anybody else for that matter, so I slithered down into the estate again, and started my search afresh. In an effort at more enquiries

I dug the snow from three front gates and waded up to three front doors, but none of them opened, although a furious dog behind one of them obviously wanted to tear me limb from limb. Only by chance did I discover St Margaret's. I rounded a wide corner across which, in an effort to beautify the scene, the council had stuck a row of those elephantine concrete pots, which, in the summer, are usually full of little dead shrubs and empty cigarette cartons. And there was the church.

My friend had said that its architect had used *great imagination*. I think he must have imagined a block. From the outside it looked just like a block, and from the inside it looked just like the same block. As I stood there gazing about me, and wondering whether the church was still in course of erection or whether it was supposed to look like that, my friend the vicar appeared from the vestry. He said he wasn't surprised that I was late, because no one ever found the church at the first attempt. And since the advent of the snow, which made it very difficult for cars to reach the place, it appeared that a large number of the regular congregation hadn't even been able to find it at all. In fact, at some services, the church had been almost empty except for a few very elderly people who hadn't got cars and came on foot.

'Mind you,' my friend continued persuasively as he conducted me up the nave, 'whatever you may think about the *architecture*' (and he knew quite well what I was thinking) 'you must admit that we have many advantages over the older churches. Our acoustics are *splendid* – no screen to muffle the sound of the choir' (I could have told him of a few people in our parish who considered that a screen was a veritable godsend in this respect) 'and of course a very effective heating system. It's all done by the touch of a switch, with electricity.' And noting that I had nearly fallen over one of the many veteran oil stoves which were scattered liberally all over the place, he explained that at the moment the whole thing seemed to have broken down, but that the contractors had given a definite guarantee that it would all be back in working order in the spring.

But some things don't change. From the vestry there suddenly rose the sound of a lone treble voice. It cheered my heart. I moved on to the next oil stove and spread my blue-cold hands in its homely, paraffin perfumed warmth, and listened. It wasn't a beautiful voice, but it reminded me happily of a pretty compliment paid to me many years ago when I was a senior choirboy. At a choir practice, a terrified probationer was running up and down the scales, and our choirmaster, as was his wont with probationers, was shuddering violently. When he could stand no more he stopped the lad and gave him some kindly words of advice and encouragement. 'If only you'd just realize what you are doing to my nerves,' he said, holding his head in his hands. 'If only you'd just *try* now and again. Now take old Frary here. When he first came he had a voice of the same remarkable paper-and-comb quality as your own, but he *tried* and now the sounds he makes are *quite* inoffensive. So do *try*!'

My friend tried to explain the voice from the vestry. 'He's a probationer,' he apologized.

'I know,' I answered.

23

Something for Everyone

'An enigma – that's what they are, an enigma,' pronounced my old friend Tim over the phone. He had
recently been installed as vicar at a not-so-small but
very remote West Country village church. After most
of a bachelor lifetime spent working in parishes in
and around London he rejoiced in anticipation of his
new, more serene lifestyle. So now he was giving me
first impressions and I'd moved him along gently,
over the overwhelmingly welcoming congregation,
the very cheerfully co-operative church wardens and
sidespersons, the delightful flower arranging ladies and
the dedicated churchyard workers and the man who
performed breathtaking acrobatic feats at the top of a
swaying ladder replacing light bulbs in almost inacces-
sible niches high in the chancel ceiling.

Then I asked him about the choir. If I could have
seen him at the other end of the phone line I'm sure
I'd have noted his brow furrow and his eyes assume a
deeply puzzled expression. 'An enigma,' he declared a
third time. 'It's like this – some Sundays they are a real
joy to listen to and sing with, then other Sundays they
sound, well, excruciating – absolutely excruciating. I

can't make them out. They are normally such lovely people.'

'As well as being such a joy and absolutely excruciating,' I concluded.

'Yes, all that as well,' he agreed. 'You must come in the choir and meet them one Sunday.'

A few weeks later I indeed found myself in the choir vestry of Tim's church preparing for Sunday morning service. Almost immediately I was greeted by a huge rumbling *basso-profundo* sound and there standing before me stood a choirman I'd known many years ago in a village church near Salisbury. We had long lost touch with each other and now expressed our immediate delight and very great surprise that we were not only still around but still active choristers. Archie still appeared to be bursting through a cassock and surplice meant for the smallest choirboy, still wore glasses with only one lens because, he said, his left eye was quite alright so didn't need any help. He seemed larger than ever and admitted that although he still rode a horse to church he had recently found a Shire horse to be more comfortable than his usual lightweight hunter.

Tim, the new vicar, ambled into the vestry, beamed at us all and explained how I came to be there this morning and how the organist came *not* to be there. 'I gather his bike is in a bit of trouble again,' he reported, 'the chain came off and flew into a ditch. He has just reconnected it so he should be with us soon. Meanwhile, we'll start the service and hope for the best with the first hymn.'

As we assembled in the choir stalls Archie said to me,

'He really ought to get a new bike y'know. There's always *something*. Last week a pedal fell off and he only just made it to play 'Here Comes the Bride' at a big wedding – he wouldn't have made it then if the bride's mother hadn't held up the whole show at the hairdresser's. They couldn't get her style just how she wanted it, y'see. Her hair didn't suit her hat. I always say a wedding service is not for the bride, it's for the bride's mother.' A large, red-faced choirlady with corrugated blue hair in the front stall turned impressively dignified and faced Archie. Did he not realize, she enquired loudly, that the service had begun and we were supposed to be singing the first hymn, not gossiping? She turned again still impressively dignified and started singing the wrong verse and the vicar smiled across at us encouragingly. The arrival of the organist during the singing of the second hymn seemed to pull us together, even inspire us and throughout the rest of the service the choir sounded good! This must have been one of their positive days described to me by Tim.

After the service and after Vicar Tim had shaken hands with every member of the congregation and some of them twice and promised to look into 'that *very* helpful suggestion', he took me off to lunch at a low tavern (well, by the look of it, it must have been low in the eighteenth century and it obviously hadn't much changed since then except that it now had electric lights heavily disguised as the original oil lamps).

We chose a large gnarled table on a sloping stone floor overlooked by a smoke-darkened oil painting of a fox dressed as a huntsman. He seemed to be grinning at our fate, probably in expectation of the sight of soup spilling freely into a guest's lap from the sloping surface.

Halfway through the low tavern's gigantic 'Special Sunday Lunch' Tim said, 'I've winkled out the riddle of the choir's alternating "joy to listen to" and "absolutely excruciating" Sunday performance.'

'Ah! A clerical detective!' I enthused 'What is the answer?'

'You no doubt noticed her in the choir this morning,' he continued, 'the lady of quite demanding presence – sat in front of you – had a few words of reprimand for Archie – often has a few words of reprimand for him. Well, at coffee after the mid-week service she was extending to me a few words of reprimand about my latest sermon regarding the meek inheriting the earth and I somehow got her onto the choir mystery and the lady explained the whole thing in a few well-chosen words. The two dominant singers in the choir are Archie the bass and young Eric the tenor. When young Eric the tenor is there everything goes smoothly as long as Archie the bass is not there. If Archie *is* there Eric sings faster and faster in an effort to get away from Archie's bellowing and make himself heard and the rest of the choir take sides as to who they will follow. If, on the other hand, Archie is there *without* Eric, the choir all follow him *en bloc* and everything sounds fine.'

'And the organist?' I asked.

Tim shrugged. 'Well, I'm told normally nobody takes any notice of what he says – he only talks about football and his bike anyway, but it's nice to have him with us because he plays such exciting voluntaries. He does a very stirring version of "The Grand March" from *Aida* just after communion. He's a very nice man, *such* a pity about his bike. If only he'd get himself a new one, but he's so *attached* to it you see. Organists seem to get attached to things – like old hymn tunes – and you often have an awful job to get them to take on new ones.'

Vicar Tim learned a lot more about his new parish in the following months. 'One thing is certain,' he told me, 'the congregation just *love* the choir. They won't hear a word against them. It seems, for instance, that I am the only one who is even slightly concerned by the descent into chaos when both Archie and young Eric are singing in the choir at the same time – well, at different times! My warden says the congregation are loyal to a fault – great traditionalists and as unmusical as the choir themselves. It's the lovely loving community spirit that keeps things going so well y'see!'

And it's the lovely, loving community spirit that keeps alive and kicking the small ancient chapel on the outskirts of the village which is also in the care of Vicar Tim and is indeed thriving these days – under the guidance of a new, young, part-time lady curate. Tim says she's a wonderful manager – musical too. She doesn't talk about forming a choir (the chapel hasn't had one for years) but talks instead about singers coming together as a church music group. She never refers to hymns – they are all praise songs. Recently she's had the coffee bar brought right into the chapel from the village hall and enlarged the formally discreet chapel notice board into an unmissable neon blaze adjoining the thatched-roofed lych-gate.

Already her invigorating crusading spirit has brought together a dedicated music group that have introduced Vivaldi into the parish for the first time in hundreds of years. It had also attracted the great interest of young Eric whose rather good tenor voice is so much better suited to Vivaldi than the village church choir's roaring Victorian choruses. In fact Eric has now wholly transfused himself from the choir to the chapel singers. Some shallow choir members say the attraction of the chapel singers for young Eric is not so much Vivaldi as the admittedly charming founder of the group but the parish's good taste firmly restricts all such ribald remarks to the choir stalls of the village church from where nowadays the choir, led unerringly by Archie's huge bass tones, can bawl their Victorian choruses gloriously unfettered by the sensitive tenor of young Eric.

As Vicar Tim happily reports, the remarkable musical differences are flourishing and the resulting enjoyment has enhanced parish unity as never before. Further, the congregations of both the church and the chapel have combined to present the village church organist with a brand new bike, and as he feels confident that the bike was foisted on him purely in the parish's loving community spirit and not because everyone is thoroughly fed up with his turning up late for Matins every other Sunday, he'll show his appreciation by using it now and again.